Most fitness programs focus on transforming the body. But, in his book Extraordinary Strength, Gio Nunemaker shows that true and lasting change will only happen when body, mind, and spirit are all transformed and then aligned under God's design. I've watched Gio live the pages of this book through seasons of triumph and trial, and I've experienced their power firsthand as both his pastor and student. The Extraordinary Strength Method™ he has created isn't just another fitness program; it's a blueprint for becoming the person God created you to be. Read this book, apply its truths, and discover the extraordinary strength that's been within you all along.

Derek Sanford
Lead Pastor, Grace Church
Author of *Untapped Church*
dereksanford.com

EXTRAORDINARY STRENGTH

Building an Unbreakable Mind, Body,
and Spirit for a Life of Purpose

GIORDANO NUNEMAKER

ISBN: 979-8-89694-629-8 - Ebook

ISBN: 979-8-89694-630-4 - Paperback

ISBN: 979-8-89694-631-1 - Hardcover

Your Free Gift–Start Your Journey Now

Before you even turn the first page...I have a gift for you.

You've picked up this book because you want more—more strength, more purpose, more faith, more life. You're not here to just *read* about extraordinary strength; you're here to *build* it.

That's why I created the Extraordinary Strength Starter Guide™—a free companion resource designed to help you take immediate action while you read.

Inside, you'll discover:

- Simple daily habits to strengthen your mind, body, and spirit

- Reflection prompts to deepen your connection with God and uncover your purpose

- A 7-day "Step into Strength" challenge to kickstart your journey right now

- Practical tools to align your life with who God created you to be

This isn't just a guide—it's your first step toward becoming the extraordinary you.

> *"God didn't create you to be ordinary. He created you*
> *to be extraordinary—in every area of your life."*

Download your free Starter Guide now at:
ExtraordinaryStrengthMethod.com/freegift

Take this first step. Begin becoming the extraordinary version of yourself today.

Live Extraordinary.

Dedication

To my mom,

You were the artistic soul, the creative heart, and the quiet strength in our family. You always dreamed of writing a book one day—a dream that stayed in your heart even when life got in the way.

Though you never had the chance to put your story on paper, your life wrote its own beautiful story through the love you gave and the courage you showed every day.

Your love, strength, and courage shaped the man I am today. Watching you face cancer with resilience and grace showed me what true strength really looks like. Your life gave this message a heartbeat.

This book is my way of carrying your dream forward—a tribute to your creative spirit, your unwavering fight, and the extraordinary strength you lived out so beautifully.

You taught me how to persevere through life's hardest challenges, to show up for others with compassion and selflessness, and to live with purpose, love, grace, and grit. Even in your own battles, you fought with a quiet strength that inspired everyone around you.

Thank you for believing in me, for inspiring me to live a life that honors the dreams we hold inside, and for showing me what it means to live an extraordinary life.

I love you, always and forever.

Table of Contents

Foreword

Most fitness books promise to change your body. Most self-help books promise to change your mind. Most spiritual books promise to change your heart. This book will change your life, because Gio Nunemaker understands what our fragmented culture has forgotten, that true transformation happens when mind, body, and spirit align. I've had the rare privilege of knowing Gio as his pastor, his student in fitness, and his fellow traveler in faith, and I can tell you that this book isn't written as theory from an armchair expert. It's a battle-tested blueprint from a man who found extraordinary strength in his darkest hour and has spent years helping others discover the same.

I've watched Gio consistently connecting his training to something greater than physical improvement. Demonstrating that caring for your fitness isn't vanity; it is stewardship. That discipline in the gym can build character for life. It was on a short-term mission trip where I truly witnessed the heart behind this book. While others focused on tasks at hand, Gio had an uncanny ability to see people, really see them. I watched him rally our team when exhaustion set in, not through rah-rah motivation, but through quiet encouragement rooted in purpose. What's more, I watched him serve the poorest of the poor with a humility that spoke louder than any motivational speech.

That's what sets this book apart. Gio has discovered what our culture desperately needs to understand: that true transformation isn't about becoming a better version of yourself for yourself; it's about becoming the person God created you to be so you can serve something and someone bigger than you.

The Extraordinary Strength Method™ you're about to encounter isn't another program promising quick fixes or easy answers. It's a comprehensive approach to human flourishing that recognizes what Scripture has always taught: we are integrated beings; mind, body, and spirit, created for purpose. When these elements align under God's design, extraordinary potential can be unleashed.

I've seen up-close-and-personal that Gio has lived these pages. He's navigated personal loss, business challenges, and the everyday struggles we all face, consistently applying the very cornerstones he outlines in this book. His authenticity shines through every page because these aren't borrowed concepts; they're battle-tested truths.

What makes this book particularly powerful is how Gio weaves together sound biblical truths with practical application. Too often, we compartmentalize our faith from our fitness, our spiritual growth from our personal development. Gio shows us that this artificial separation limits our potential. When we approach transformation holistically, aligning our thoughts with God's designs, we discover strength we never knew we possessed.

The stories you'll read aren't meant to impress you with Gio's genius, but to awaken you to your own possibilities. From his own journey through depression and purposelessness to his mother's courageous battle with cancer, from the three-year-old he helped overcome physical limitations to his grandparents thriving in their eighties, these stories reveal a profound truth: extraordinary strength isn't reserved for a select few. It's available to anyone willing to do the work of aligning their life with God's design.

As you embark on this journey, you'll find practical tools, biblical wisdom, and honest encouragement. You'll also find something rarer: a guide who understands that lasting change requires more than information, it requires transformation from the inside out.

The world doesn't need another person who's simply stronger, smarter, or more successful. The world needs people who've discovered their extraordinary purpose and have the strength of mind, body, and spirit to live it out. That's what this book offers. That's what Gio embodies. And that's what I believe God wants to awaken in you.

Get ready to discover the extraordinary strength that's been within you all along.

Derek Sanford
Lead Pastor, Grace Church
Author of *Untapped Church*
dereksanford.com

The Foundation of Extraordinary Strength

The Power of Purpose

"And we know that for those who love God all things work together for good, for those who are called according to His purpose." - Romans 8:28

What if everything you've been through—every hardship, failure, setback, and victory—wasn't random? What if it was preparing you for something greater?

I believe it was. Because I've lived it. I've battled through depression, questioned my strength, and wrestled with identity. I've felt disconnected—strong in one area of life, but crumbling in others. I was once the guy who looked fit on the outside but was falling apart mentally and spiritually on the inside.

I tried to muscle my way through life with discipline alone, but I was missing the bigger picture.

What I learned through it all is this: true strength is not built in the absence of struggle. It is forged in it. And it's not just physical strength. Extraordinary strength—the kind that endures—is built from the inside out.

It begins in the mind.

It's sustained in the body.

It's powered by the Spirit.

And it's ignited through Purpose.

This book is a guide for the person who wants more out of life— not just better fitness, more energy, or greater discipline (though you'll gain those too)—but lasting transformation that is rooted in something deeper. It's the journey I had to take when I realized I was strong in the gym but weak where it mattered most—inside my mind, my heart, and my spirit.

This is a book for the person who wants to live with intention, with direction, and with a sense of meaning that goes beyond the surface.

You were created for something extraordinary. And whether you feel strong right now or like you're barely holding it together, I believe this journey will equip you with the tools, truths, and habits to become who God created you to be—mentally, physically, spiritually, and purposefully.

I challenge you to commit to this journey. By the time you finish this book, you will not be the same person who started it.

Are you ready? Let's begin.

Introducing The Extraordinary Strength Method™

The Extraordinary Strength Method™ is a faith-based, four-phase transformation method built to help you become strong in the areas that matter most. It is not just about fitness—it's about aligning your whole life with God's purpose for you.

This is the method I built when I was at a breaking point—when I needed more than just motivation or muscle. I needed a map for renewal. One that addressed the whole person—mind, body, spirit, and purpose.

It is built upon four cornerstones:

- Master Your Mind—Mental Strength
- Strengthen Your Body—Physical Strength
- Awaken Your Spirit—Spiritual Strength
- Forge Your Purpose—Purposeful Living

Each cornerstone supports powerful pillars—habits and principles that develop character, discipline, faith, and alignment. And each builds upon the last, bringing you deeper into your calling and more fully into the extraordinary version of you that God designed.

Let me be clear: this is not a quick fix. This is the process that saved my life, and it could transform yours, too.

This is a lifelong process. But as you walk through each cornerstone, you'll learn how to:

- Replace limiting beliefs with unshakable confidence
- Build a body that supports your mission and honors God

- Deepen your faith and discover the power of spiritual connection

- Align your life with your God-given purpose and step into your why

The Cornerstones at a Glance

1. Master Your Mind

The foundation.

Your transformation begins here. Your thoughts shape your actions, and your actions shape your life. Without mental strength, everything else crumbles.

I know this firsthand—when I was at my lowest, it wasn't my body that failed me, it was my mindset.

I was stuck in self-doubt, repeating old patterns, and believing lies about who I was and what I was capable of. It wasn't until I took full ownership of my thoughts and began renewing my mind through Scripture and intentional practice that real change began.

You must first conquer the thoughts that try to convince you that you're not enough. This cornerstone will teach you how to build mental resilience, overcome self-doubt, take responsibility for your life, and embrace the daily discomforts that lead to growth.

Because if you don't win the battle in your mind, you'll never step into the life God has for you.

2. Strengthen Your Body

The vehicle.

Your body is the vessel through which you live out your purpose. When disciplined, fueled, and trained properly, it becomes a tool.

As a coach, I've spent years training others—but for a long time, I ignored what my own health was saying back to me. I was running on empty, burning out while looking "fit."

Once I aligned my physical training with God's purpose—not just for performance but for stewardship—it shifted everything. My energy, my confidence, and my ability to lead all changed.

Discipline starts in the body. You'll learn how training, nutrition, and self-control impact far more than your appearance—they influence your energy, your leadership, your family, and your ability to live out your calling.

3. Awaken Your Spirit

The power source.

Faith is your power source. Without the Spirit, all your strength leads to striving.

For years, I tried to push forward on grit alone—but something was always missing. When I finally surrendered, I realized I had been fighting battles in my own strength instead of tapping into God's. That's when everything began to shift.

This section will guide you in building a stronger connection to God, uncovering the fruits of the Spirit, deepening your relationships, serving with intention, and greater clarity of heart. This is where passion meets purpose and joy meets peace. Here, you'll be reminded that you were never meant to walk this road alone.

4. Forge Your Purpose

The direction.

Finally, we bring everything together. Purpose gives meaning to the mind, body, and spirit. Without it, you may build strength—but not significance.

I've seen what happens when someone trains hard, grows disciplined, and builds faith—but still lacks direction. I've lived that story. Purpose is what gives all your effort meaning.

This is where you'll identify your unique calling, confront the fears holding you back, and align your mind, body, and spirit to walk boldly in the purpose God designed for you. This is where you stop living on autopilot—and start living with intention.

The Cornerstones Work Together

These four cornerstones are not separate paths. They are interdependent. Each one builds upon and supports the others. Miss one, and the whole structure is weakened.

A Unified Vision of Strength:

- **Mind**: The foundation that shapes everything else

- **Body**: The vehicle that executes what the mind envisions

- **Spirit**: The power source that sustains both mind and body

- **Purpose**: The direction that gives meaning to all three

The Consequences of Missing a Cornerstone

- **Strong Mind but weak Body** = Vision without execution

  - You might have clarity. You might know your purpose. You might dream big. But without the physical energy and strength to act, those dreams stay dreams. Your potential stalls out at the starting line, and frustration builds as your mind races ahead of a body that can't keep up.

- **Strong Body but weak Mind** = Action without direction

  - You're moving, grinding, doing all the things—but without purpose or clarity. You become a high-performing machine, burning energy without fulfillment. You may achieve outward success, but inside, you feel aimless. You confuse motion with progress, but something always feels… off.

- **Strong Mind and Body but weak Spirit** = Burnout and emptiness

  - You have the mindset. You have the discipline. You built the habits. But if your spirit isn't anchored in something greater, you will burn out. Without God's presence and guidance, you begin to rely entirely on yourself—and that weight becomes too heavy to carry. The result? Emptiness. Exhaustion. And the haunting question: *What's the point of all this?*

- **All three without Purpose** = Strength without impact
  - Even if your mind is sharp, your body is strong, and your spirit is steady—without purpose, it all stays self-contained. You may be impressive, but you're not impactful. You were made to live for something greater than yourself. Without that mission, your strength becomes hollow—a performance instead of a legacy.

I've lived out each of those imbalances. I've seen the consequences of neglecting one area. That's why this method was born—out of necessity, out of pain, and ultimately, out of God's grace.

This is why the Extraordinary Strength Method™ doesn't just train the body, or build the mind, or strengthen the spirit in isolation. It aligns them—because God designed you to be whole.

Extraordinary strength comes only when all four are integrated.

This book will show you how.

How to Use This Book

Each chapter is packed with Scripture, story, action steps, reflection questions, and truth. Don't rush it. Don't skip around. Let each section build upon the last. This journey is designed the same way I had to walk it—one step at a time, one battle at a time—with God at the center.

There was a season when I wanted quick answers and surface-level motivation. I tried to patch up the outside without addressing what was broken within. But true transformation doesn't come that way.

This method was built in the trenches—through trial, through grace, and through the daily decision to get back up.

Throughout the book, you'll find:

- Real-life stories that connect to your own struggles and victories

- Biblical truths that offer hope and direction

- Habits and practices that build momentum in daily life

- A method you can apply for life—not just for a season

These are the same habits that helped me crawl out of burnout, reclaim my joy, and rediscover who God created me to be.

Transformation requires consistent action. Throughout this book, each cornerstone and pillar will provide specific actionable steps to help you develop mental resilience, physical strength, and spiritual growth. Your commitment to applying these steps will determine your success in building extraordinary strength.

By following this method, you'll not only transform your own life but become a leader who inspires and uplifts others.

The Extraordinary Life Awaits

By the end of this book, you won't just know more—you'll be more. You'll be stronger in mind, body, and spirit. You'll know your purpose, live it with passion, and walk in the extraordinary strength God has already placed within you.

I don't know exactly where you're starting—but I know what it's like to start from a place of emptiness, confusion, or frustration. And I know what it's like to build a life of joy, strength, and clarity—by the grace of God and one faithful step at a time.

This is your invitation.

Not just to read—but to transform.

Not just to learn—but to live.

Not just to survive—but to thrive in the purpose God uniquely placed in you.

Are you ready to become the extraordinary you God created you to be?

Let's begin.

Awakening Extraordinary Strength

Before we dive into your transformation, I want to share mine. Because this method wasn't born from theory—it was born in the trenches of fear, failure, and faith.

Finding Purpose Through Struggle

Before you can build strength in your body, mind, and spirit, you have to discover what you're building it for.

The Search for Purpose

Mark Twain once said, *"The two most important days in your life are the day you are born and the day you find out why."* Viktor Frankl echoed this truth: *"Those who have a 'why' to live, can bear with almost any 'how.'"*

Have you ever laid awake at night, staring at the ceiling, asking yourself, *"What is my purpose? Why am I here? What happens when I die?"* If you have, you're not alone.

I've asked those questions in the darkest moments of my life—when I felt lost, uncertain, or crushed by the weight of pain. But once I began to understand my purpose—everything changed. The pain didn't disappear. The struggles didn't stop. But I no longer walked through life aimlessly. I had direction. I had hope. I had a purpose.

But finding that purpose wasn't easy. It didn't happen all at once. It was a messy, painful journey that nearly ended before it ever began. But looking back, I can see it clearly now:

Every struggle, every setback, every moment of doubt was forging in me a strength I didn't yet understand.

A strength that would become the foundation of my mission, my faith, and ultimately—this book.

The truth is—your greatest strength is often found in your greatest struggles.

This first part of the book is my journey. Not because my story is special, but because it might mirror parts of your own. And if it does, my prayer is that it will light a spark within you—to pursue the extraordinary purpose you were created for.

That's why I wrote this, not just to tell my story, but to walk with you through your own. This book will guide you through the process of developing extraordinary strength—in your Mind. In your Body. In your Spirit. And ultimately, in your Purpose.

Because purpose is not just a feel-good idea. It's the cornerstone of everything.

That's why we start here—with my journey. I want you to see that even when you're lost, broken, or unsure of what's next… God is working.

He's shaping something powerful in you. He's preparing you for a greater calling.

So as you read this part of my story, don't just observe—reflect. Where are you now in your own search for purpose?

What trials have been shaping you without you realizing it?

We'll explore purpose more fully later as a cornerstone of this book, but for now, I want you to see the beginning of where that purpose was born in me.

Not in success, but in brokenness.

A Dream Shattered

As a teenager, I was obsessed with football. I lived and breathed the game. It wasn't just something I played—it was part of who I was. I dreamed of playing in college, maybe even beyond. But then, one conversation changed everything.

"You'll never play in college. You're too small." That's what my coach told me.

Just like that, my dream was shattered. I had no backup plan, no sense of direction. If football wasn't my future, what was?

At that age, I didn't have the tools to process that kind of loss. So, I did what many do—I followed the crowd. My friends had chosen Sports Management as their college major, so I followed them thinking I would still find a way to be in the sports world. But when we attended orientation, something hit me: *I hated it.*

I looked around at my friends, who were excited about this new chapter, and realized I didn't feel the same way. They decided to stick with it, but I knew I needed something different. I felt... lost.

That's when I thought about my elementary school gym teacher. He was one of the most positive, inspiring people I had ever met. He made every kid feel like they mattered, regardless of their athletic ability. He didn't just teach gym—he built confidence, resilience, and belief in every student.

I wanted to be like that. I wanted to impact people the way he impacted me. So, I switched my major to health and physical education, thinking I had finally found my purpose. But the real journey was just beginning.

When Life Falls Apart

My first year of college went great. I finished with a 4.0 GPA. I was thriving—at least on the surface.

Then, I made a decision that changed everything.

There was a girl. She was my world. My life revolved around her, in ways that, looking back, weren't healthy. When I transferred to a school closer to home so I could be with her, I convinced myself it was the right move. But when the relationship ended, my entire world came crashing down.

I didn't just lose a relationship—I lost myself.

I fell into a dark place. I stopped working out. I drank constantly. I no longer cared about school, my future, or even my own well-being. My GPA plummeted. But worse than that, I stopped caring whether I lived or died.

Almost every night, I drank until I felt numb. And when the numbness wasn't enough, I turned to self-harm. I was trapped in a darkness I didn't think I'd ever escape.

I was trapped in a cycle of pain and destruction. And then, one night, as I stood on the edge of a life-altering decision, fear gripped me. Not of just death, but of wasting my life.

"Do I really want my story to end this way?"

Somewhere deep inside, a whisper cut through the chaos: "You were made for more."

Fighting My Way Back

That moment didn't fix everything overnight, but it was the turning point. The next day, I reached out to friends. I started taking antidepressants. I slowly began to rebuild... brick by brick.

The gym became my lifeline.

At first, I worked out for revenge. *"I'll get in the best shape of my life, and she'll regret leaving me."* But revenge is weak fuel. It burns out fast.

Thankfully, I had friends who kept me accountable. They dragged me to the gym when I didn't want to go. They didn't let me give up. And somewhere along the way, lifting weights became something more—it became therapy. It became clear. It became strength in every sense of the word.

Studies confirm what I experienced firsthand—resistance training improves mental health. It reduces depression, anxiety, and improves your ability to process life's challenges. My workouts weren't just changing my body—they were rebuilding my mind and restoring my spirit.

And what I didn't know then was that all of this was forging something much deeper inside of me...

A mission.

A calling.

A purpose.

Discovering Passion and Calling

A Broken System

The deeper I went into my journey, the more I realized something: our system is broken.

At first, I thought my purpose was to be a gym teacher—to impact the next generation and give them the confidence and strength that my own gym teacher had helped instill in me. But when I stepped into the education system, I quickly saw how misaligned it was with the mission on my heart.

Instead of pushing students to become their best, many schools lower the bar. I saw kids being rewarded for just showing up—not for putting in effort, challenging themselves, or growing. Physical education wasn't about building strength, discipline, or resilience—it was about keeping things safe, fair, and watered-down.

That's not life. Life doesn't hand you gold stars for mediocrity. It punches you in the gut and expects you to get back up.

Too often, we lower standards so that no one feels left out or uncomfortable. But what about the kids who want to be challenged? What about the ones who need that push to realize what they're capable of?

I realized something important: mediocrity isn't just tolerated—it's celebrated. If gym class isn't physically challenging, how can we expect kids to value movement? If we're not pushing them mentally or physically, what are we preparing them for?

We are all made to be great at something. But if no one challenges us to find that greatness and grow it, how can we ever become who we were made to be? Without discomfort, there's no development. Without resistance, there's no strength. If we aren't prepared for life's challenges while we're young, how will we handle them when they come full force in adulthood?

That system wasn't for me. I knew I couldn't thrive—or help others thrive—within a structure that celebrated average. I wasn't called to keep people comfortable. I was called to help people grow.

I knew that if I stayed, I would become frustrated, complacent, and eventually burnt out. And worse—I wouldn't be helping people unlock their full potential. That's when I started searching for something more.

Finding My True Passion

That's when I found Exercise Science. My friends and family thought I was crazy. *"What are you going to do? Be a personal trainer? That's not a real career."* But I didn't care. I had seen firsthand how fitness saved my life, and I knew I needed to help others experience that same breakthrough.

I graduated, got off my antidepressants, and landed a job at a gym. At first, I thought my path was training elite athletes. It made sense—those were the people who cared about performance, who pushed themselves.

So I did my best to make a name for myself within this facility and train as many people as possible. But then, something unexpected happened: I started working with everyday people—people who doubted themselves, who walked in thinking they were broken, who believed they could never change.

And I saw something beautiful happen.

For most of them, working out was a huge step in their health, and they really needed guidance and encouragement to make changes in their life. Most believed that they couldn't do it. That they could not make changes in their life.

Well, when those changes started to happen, their excitement and joy was intoxicating! They started seeing that they could do way more than they thought and seeing their changes brought me true joy.

When someone who thought they weren't capable finally lifted a weight they didn't think they could… when they ran farther than ever before… when they started smiling at their reflection instead of criticizing it—something shifted in me.

I started to see that this is who I wanted to work with. I realized these were the people I wanted to serve. Those that were struggling to believe in themselves. I connected with that and what I had gone through. I wanted to show them that they could not only make it through their challenges, but turn their challenges into opportunities, just like I had. I wanted to share that with others. I knew it could impact others and change their lives as well, just like it had mine.

I was starting to find my purpose! Athletes already believed in themselves. But the people who walked in doubting their potential, unsure of their strength—they were the ones who needed me the most.

Helping people go from hopeless to hopeful… from weak to strong… from lost to found—that became my real "why."

I wasn't just helping people get fit. I was helping them discover who they truly were. That was the beginning of my deeper purpose: to show people how they could become the extraordinary version of themselves, just like I had to learn.

The Fire That Ignited My Mission

A year into my career, I attended a Perform Better Seminar. The world's best strength and conditioning coaches, personal trainers, and business owners went to these and taught at these seminars.

I learned so much from so many great coaches, but there was one man that truly inspired me: Martin Rooney. His energy was contagious. He didn't just train people—he changed lives. He introduced me to

Training for Warriors (TFW), a program built on mind, body, and spirit—something I had never seen before.

At that moment, I knew I had found something special. I went expecting to learn about training. I left with a mission.

I took the idea back to my gym. They weren't interested. So I left.

At the same time, I was training at a local facility where the owner and manager—Scott Faulkner and DJ Myers—were looking to bring on new trainers. I pitched them my vision, and to my surprise, they leaned in.

Within a year, I became part-owner along with DJ. We rebranded as Erie Fitness Academy and launched TFW South Erie. It was a game-changer. Lives were being transformed—physically, mentally, and spiritually. It was more than a gym—it was a mission field.

We weren't just helping people lose weight or lift heavier. We were building warriors—people equipped to overcome life's battles. We were using the gym as a tool to transform people in every area: mind, body, and spirit.

I wasn't just a trainer anymore. I was a Coach. A guide. A vessel for transformation.

But as powerful as that was, something was still missing.

Faith—The Missing Piece

The Final Piece—Faith

Around that time, I was pursuing someone I deeply cared about— spoiler alert: she's now my wife. Early in that time, she said something that stopped me in my tracks: "I want a man who has a relationship with God."

I had grown up as a Christian, but after everything I had been through, I had turned away. I called myself an atheist. But the truth is, I didn't stop believing in God—I was angry with Him. And how can you hate something you claim not to believe in?

I started going to church just to impress her. But something strange happened. Every sermon spoke directly to me. The same principles I applied in fitness—discipline, consistency, pushing past pain for a greater purpose—were all in scripture. It all lined up with faith in a way I had never noticed before. The more I listened, the more I saw the connection between training and faith.

One day, I couldn't deny it anymore. I got down on my knees and rededicated my life to Christ. And suddenly, the missing piece fell into place. Suddenly, everything made sense.

I had the passion. I had the platform. Now, I have the foundation.

Fitness wasn't my purpose. Coaching wasn't my purpose.

Helping people become who God made them to be—that was my purpose.

And it would become the foundation for everything else.

Those nights wondering what life was all about and if life meant anything at all were gone. I was able to see how the struggles in my life were leading me to this point. How those struggles helped shape me and had great lessons in them that I did not see during the time.

I saw purpose to it all, and I found my purpose in life through it. God purposefully put all the challenges I have been through to get me to this spot in my life right now where I am writing this book.

It wasn't random. It was preparation. It was for a purpose.

My calling wasn't just to help people get fit. My calling was to help people rebuild their strength from the inside out—mind, body, and spirit. My mission wasn't just physical. It was eternal.

> *"And we know that for those who love God all things work together for good, for those who are called according to his purpose."* —Romans 8:28 (ESV)

Your Extraordinary Journey Begins

Why This Book?

If you're reading this, you're searching for something, too. Maybe it's purpose. Maybe it's faith. Maybe it's just a way to push through the challenges in front of you. Whether you believe in God or not, the lessons in this book apply to everyone.

You might feel stuck. Overwhelmed. Maybe even lost. And I get that. I've been there too. But I need you to know this: there is more in you than you could ever imagine.

This book isn't about six-packs or motivational quotes. It's about building the kind of strength that lasts—Extraordinary Strength.

The kind that helps you fight through pain.

The kind that helps you find peace in the chaos.

The kind that equips you to live out your purpose, no matter what life throws your way.

This is the journey to becoming the person God created you to be—through mastering your mind, strengthening your body, awakening your spirit, and ultimately discovering your purpose.

That's what this book is here to guide you through:

- A mind equipped with clarity, discipline, and grit.
- A body built to serve with strength and energy.
- A spirit anchored in faith and divine connection.
- A purpose that pulls you forward through every season.

But make no mistake—this isn't about becoming someone else.

It's about becoming the extraordinary version of you that God designed from the beginning.

The version of you who is equipped to make the impact only you can make.

And no matter where you're starting, how many times you've fallen, or how far you feel from your potential—this journey meets you where you are and walks with you forward, one cornerstone and one pillar at a time.

And by the end of this journey, when you've renewed your mind, strengthened your body, and awakened your spirit, you'll return to the place where it all started.

Purpose.

Only this time, you won't be searching for it.

You'll be living it.

Are you ready to discover your Extraordinary Strength?

Together, we'll explore the parallels between faith and fitness, uncover your why, and take action to transform every aspect of your life.

This journey won't be easy. But I promise you—it will be worth it. As Martin Rooney says, "Your past does not determine your future." The challenges you face today are opportunities for growth. We will use your past and present to become the best versions of yourself moving forward!

It's time to step up and become the person God created you to be; the extraordinary you. Are you ready for extraordinary strength? Let's begin where all things start: Your Mind.

You got this! Let's go.

Master Your Mind (Mental Strength)

Pillar 1: Belief

Conquer Yourself—Renewing Your Mind

You've begun uncovering your purpose—the spark that drives everything else.

Now it's time to build the mental strength to carry it forward.

This won't be easy. Real growth never is. But with the right mindset, every obstacle becomes an opportunity, and every challenge becomes a stepping stone toward the extraordinary.

We begin with the mind because this is where transformation starts— or where it stops.

Before you can strengthen your body or awaken your spirit, you must first take control of the thoughts that shape your reality.

You must learn to break free from self-doubt, fear, and limiting beliefs.

Because no matter how clear your purpose is, if your mind isn't ready, you'll never pursue it with confidence.

It's time to train your mind to believe, to focus, and to fight. It's time to conquer yourself.

You are your own greatest obstacle. When you feel called to something greater, your mind starts racing. You tell yourself you're not ready, not qualified, not enough. But those thoughts—the self-limiting beliefs, the fear of failure, the struggle with discipline and discomfort—don't define you. They're your old self. And it's time to leave it behind.

> *"To put off your old self, which belongs to your former manner of life and is corrupt through deceitful desires, and to be renewed in the spirit of your minds… to put on the new self, created after the likeness of God in true righteousness and holiness."* —*Ephesians 4:22-24 (ESV)*

True transformation begins in the mind. *"I appeal to you therefore, brothers, by the mercies of God, to present your bodies as a living sacrifice, holy and acceptable to God, which is your spiritual worship. Do not be conformed to this world, but be transformed by the renewal of your mind, that by testing you may discern what is the will of God, what is good and acceptable and perfect."* —Romans 12:1-2 (ESV)

In this cornerstone, we're going to uncover the patterns, habits, and thoughts that have been holding you back—and replace them with strength, truth, and purpose.

Because before you can fully step into your God-given mission, you must confront and overcome the biggest barrier in your path: Yourself.

Breaking Free from Self-Doubt

Throughout high school and college, I never saw myself as much. I had little self-confidence, struggled with self-worth, and had a hard time making friends and connecting with people because I always thought they didn't like me.

I tried being like other people but always felt off center, so I would be sort of like them. It always put me in a weird spot, trying to be different from who I was made to be, not being my authentic self. But when my mind kept on telling me that people wouldn't like the real me, I wouldn't act like myself.

Trying to be someone I wasn't slowly wore me down. I didn't notice it at first, but I was constantly drained—mentally, emotionally, even physically. I'd walk into rooms wondering who I needed to be for people to like me, always adjusting, never fully settled. After that high-school-into-college relationship ended, I didn't just feel sad—I unraveled. That relationship was the only place I let my guard down and felt like I could be myself.

So when it ended, it felt like the ground gave out underneath me. I stopped showing up—socially, academically, even spiritually. I isolated myself, skipped class, slept all the time, and constantly replayed every conversation in my head, wondering what I did wrong. I'd stare at my phone, hoping for a text that never came, then beat myself up for caring so much. I couldn't even look people in the eye. I avoided friends, meals, mirrors. I didn't just feel sad—I felt worthless. I didn't know who I was without her, because I had never learned to be okay with who I was in the first place. And the truth was, I had never built a foundation of belief in myself, so when that one connection disappeared, everything I had leaned on came crashing down.

Looking back, I can absolutely see why it didn't work out. I was so reliant on that person that they held that entire weight of my happiness on them. That was just way too much for them to have to carry, and it was a recipe for disaster.

So when it was over, it was like my happiness died. I had never taken the time to build the mental structures to defeat my own self talk or believe in myself. When my college friends got me out of my own way, showed that they believed in me, it got me to start taking the right actions to better myself, believe in myself, and put on a new self by the renewal of my mind.

Henry Ford once said, "Whether you think you can or can't, you're right." And for the longest time, I thought I couldn't. I was right, because my mindset made it so. That quote hit home for me, because it revealed a truth I had lived without knowing: your belief determines your direction.

Many of us live like elephants tied to a rope—restrained by experiences that no longer have power over us. We let past failures define our future potential, never realizing that we are free to break loose. But when we break free from these false beliefs, we step into our God-given potential.

Cutting the Mental Chains That Hold You Back

Here is one of my favorite motivational stories that we have received from Training for Warriors by an unknown author:

"As my friend was passing the elephants, he suddenly stopped, confused by the fact that these huge creatures were being held by only a small rope tied to their front legs. No chains, no cages. It was obvious that the elephants could, at any time, break away from the ropes they were tied to but for some reason, they did not. My friend saw a trainer nearby and asked why these beautiful, magnificent animals just stood there and made no attempt to get away.

"Well," he said, "when they were very young and much smaller, we used the same size of rope to tie them and, at that age, it's enough to hold them. As they grew up, they were conditioned to believe they cannot break away. They believe the rope can still hold them, so they never try to break free." My friend was amazed. These animals could at any time break free from their bonds, but because they believed they couldn't, they were stuck right where they were."

These giant elephants could break free at any time, but because they didn't believe that they could —because it was not able to before— they quit trying and had no belief that it was even possible. They let their past determine their future. They let an old failure dictate their mindset and their future. Their self-limiting belief stopped them from becoming the greatest version of themselves.

Belief will either propel you forward or keep you stuck. To step into your extraordinary purpose, you must strengthen your faith in God and yourself. Your mind is a wonderful and powerful thing, but when left uncontrolled, it can be devastating. If you are anything like I was or if you are like the elephants from the story, there is a mental shift that has to happen to get to the most extraordinary version of you. A big part of that shift is the belief that you have in yourself, your purpose, and God. You are "fearfully and wonderfully made" by God,

Psalm 139:14, to do extraordinary things. But if you don't believe it, the promptings by others and even by the Holy Spirit won't get you there.

Most go through life trapped by their own self-limiting beliefs that they are not capable of becoming something more than they are, that they can't make more money, have that dream job, get out of that bad relationship, break the family cycle, get sober, or even to get healthy. They let their life circumstances and even their past dictate their future. One of the first things is letting go of the past. Letting go of the things that are holding you back. You have to cut that rope and start taking the right actions to move forward. Just because you were not successful in the past does not mean you cannot be successful now. Your past does not determine your future, the actions that you take today do!

Cutting those ties might be getting rid of negative and toxic relationships. Just because someone or a group of people have been in your life for a while does not mean they are going to be with you for the rest of your life. Some people are seasonal, that is okay. You cannot take everyone with you. If you are trying to grow and become better, and they are holding you back and not wanting to grow themselves, it is okay to move on from them. It does not mean you cannot ever be around them, but it is time to find a new circle of people. If there are people that are doing what you want to do and growing themselves and others around them, it is time to get in that room and surround yourself with those people and people on the same mission as you.

It's like someone that is trying to become sober and they quit drinking. Every time they go out with their "drinking buddies," it is going to be nearly impossible for them not to drink. That's why they call them "drinking buddies" because that's all that they do together. If you are trying to get healthier but the people around you eat and drink junk, are not active, and don't want to change for the better, they will actually try to pull you back into bad habits with them and sabotage your own belief that you can make that change for yourself. When you are making better and healthier changes in your life, they will see all the things that they are not willing to do and try to guilt you into going back, telling you how you can't do it, all because you are making them feel bad about themselves. Well, if they are not willing to take those steps with you, you have to move on without them. You cannot surround yourself with people that want to drag you back into their bad habits and ways and bring you down instead of building you up. It's okay, it doesn't mean they will not get to that point to want to change, you just cannot wait for them to get there. You have to start taking those steps now.

Like the elephants, many of us remain stuck—not because we are incapable, but because we believe we are. Your past does not determine your future. The actions you take today do.

How to Break Free:

- **Recognize the Lies**: Identify the limiting beliefs that have shaped your decisions.

- **Challenge the Narrative**: Replace self-doubt with God's truth about who you are.

- **Surround Yourself with the Right People**: Community shapes confidence. Find people who encourage growth.

- **Take Action Despite Fear**: Courage isn't the absence of fear; it's moving forward anyway.

You are *"fearfully and wonderfully made"*—Psalm 139:14 (ESV) for a greater purpose. The question is—do you believe it?

The Power of Belief

Have you ever felt called to something greater—but doubted whether you could actually do it? Maybe you've set a goal, dreamed of change, or felt God stirring something in you, but your first thought was, *"Not me. I'm not ready. I don't have what it takes."*

If so, you're not alone. Belief doesn't come naturally to most people—it's built.

Belief is the fuel that drives transformation. Without belief, even the best intentions, plans, and dreams will falter. But here's the good news: belief isn't something you're either born with or without. It's something you can train. Just like muscles grow through training, your belief grows through intentional practice and action.

That's why The Extraordinary Strength Method™ includes belief as a core foundation—because without belief, nothing else works.

And belief isn't just theory—it's proven.

For decades, running a mile in under four minutes was considered physically impossible. Medical experts and scientists claimed the human heart would explode from the effort. This belief was so ingrained that despite many elite athletes training specifically for this goal, no one could break through the barrier.

Then on May 6, 1954, Roger Bannister did the "impossible"—he ran a mile in 3 minutes and 59.4 seconds.

What followed was even more astonishing. Within just 46 days of Bannister's achievement, Australian runner John Landy also broke the four-minute barrier. Within three years, 16 other runners had done the same. Today, even high school athletes have joined that list.

What changed wasn't human physiology. What changed was belief.

This story powerfully illustrates the principles behind this pillar:

- Limiting beliefs create real barriers – What we believe to be impossible becomes impossible for us.

- Breakthrough beliefs create cascade effects – Once Bannister broke through, others quickly followed because the "impossible" became possible in their minds.

- Belief precedes physical reality – The primary obstacle wasn't physical capability but mental limitation.

- Community belief matters – When one person demonstrates something is possible, it changes what an entire community believes they can achieve.

This isn't just a motivational story—it's spiritual truth.

The Bible tells us, *"For as he thinketh in his heart, so is he."* – Proverbs 23:7 (KJV)

Transformation begins in the mind before it manifests in the body or in our circumstances.

This is why mastering belief is non-negotiable. You can't live out God's purpose for your life while carrying a mindset of defeat. When you believe in what's possible, you begin to act in alignment with your calling. You begin to train like it, eat like it, live like it, and speak like it.

The four-minute mile is no longer a barrier. It's a reminder that the only limits that hold us back are the ones we choose to accept.

So what's your "four-minute mile"?

What barrier do you need to stop calling impossible?

Your belief—fueled by truth, faith, and action—can shatter it.

Because belief is where extraordinary strength begins.

The Role of Belief in Transformation

Belief is the bridge between intention and action.

- What you believe about yourself determines how you show up daily.
- Belief in God's purpose for your life keeps you anchored during tough times.
- Belief fuels the discipline to keep going when motivation runs dry.

If you believe that change is possible, you'll keep taking steps forward. If you believe God has equipped you, you'll walk in confidence.

Reflection Questions: Building a Strong Mental Foundation

Take time to journal or think deeply about these questions. Belief starts by confronting the thoughts that are shaping your life today.

- What are the beliefs about yourself that are currently shaping your thoughts and actions?

- Are those beliefs aligned with who God says you are?

- How can you replace limiting beliefs with empowering truths from Scripture?

- What affirmations or verses can you repeat daily to reinforce belief in your God-given potential?

Habits to Build Belief

You don't need to "feel" belief before you act on it. You build belief by practicing it daily. Here are habits to start right now:

- Daily Affirmations: Speak positive, truth-based affirmations over your life. Choose 1–3 that resonate and say them aloud every day, such as:
  - "I am capable of change."
  - "God has a plan for my life."
  - *"I can do all things through him who strengthens me."* — Philippians 4:13 (ESV)

- Scripture Study: Meditate on verses that reinforce belief in God's purpose for you. Suggested verses:

- Jeremiah 29:11

- Philippians 4:13

- Visualization: Spend five minutes each day visualizing yourself living out your purpose. Picture yourself succeeding in your goals. See yourself taking action with confidence and courage.

- Surround Yourself with Believers: Engage with a community of like-minded individuals who inspire belief. Your circle either builds your belief or tears it down. Choose wisely.

Bringing It Together: Belief in Action

Belief is not just a feeling—it's a practice. It's a decision to stand on God's promises even when you don't feel strong. *"Faith is the assurance of things hoped for, the conviction of things not seen."* —Hebrews 11:1 (ESV)

You may not feel ready, but you don't have to. You are already equipped through Christ. Your job is to train your belief like a muscle—daily, intentionally, consistently. And that's exactly what The Extraordinary Strength Method™ will help you do. You'll learn how to build an unshakable belief that powers every area of your life.

So let me ask you:

- What's one small action you can take today to strengthen your belief?

- What limiting thought will you replace with truth?

Start today—because belief is the foundation for becoming the extraordinary you. Building belief is like building a muscle—it grows as you use it. But as you step forward in belief, there's one obstacle that almost always shows up: fear of failure.

I've seen it in my own life, and I see it in the people I coach. Just when you start to believe you're made for more, fear creeps in and says, "What if I mess this up? What if I fail?"

But what if I told you that failure isn't something to be avoided—but embraced? What if failure is actually part of God's training ground for your greatness?

That's exactly where we're going next: into the truth about failure, and why it's not the end, but a beginning.

Final Charge: Believe It or Stay Bound

Your belief is the first battle you must win. Before you can build your body, sharpen your skills, or walk in purpose, you must first win the war in your mind.

You can't wait for belief to magically show up—you build it through daily action. By showing up when you don't feel like it. By speaking truth when lies creep in. By choosing faith when fear whispers in your ear. You were created for extraordinary things—but you'll never live them out unless you believe it.

So what will you choose? Will you stay stuck in the chains of self-doubt, fear, and limiting beliefs? Or will you break free, cut the rope, and step boldly into the person God has called you to be?

This is your moment. Believe it. Live it. Step forward in faith—because the extraordinary life you were created for is waiting.

Pillar 2: Fear of Failure

Fear of Failure—Why Failing is Your Greatest Teacher

Along with your belief about yourself, you have to be willing to fail. Many that have a hard time believing in their own abilities failed at something in the past, and that is how they now identify themselves–as failures. Failing is not a bad thing. You just learned the way not to do something. Awesome! That's progress! Failing is not the end, it is the beginning of something amazing. Many people fear failure, but failure is not the enemy—it is the greatest opportunity for growth. Failure is not the opposite of success—it is the process of success.

> *"For though the righteous fall seven times, they rise again."* — *Proverbs 24:16 (NIV)*

When we are training people in our gym, we have those that have trained enough to work up to a one rep max in that lift, which is the heaviest you can do for that lift for one rep. We do this for many reasons, but the main purpose is to see where they fail.

Yes, we absolutely want them to fail at the lift!

If they don't fail, it is not a true test, since we did not find their maximum strength in that lift. We want to see and want them to see what they are truly capable of. This is such a great gift, especially when you don't believe in your own abilities. Then, with some coaching and encouragement, they end up astonished at how strong they truly are.

Sure, they failed at it, but now they know their maximum strength in that lift and more importantly, where they failed. That's extremely important because now it gives us, and them, information for the next step and what we are going to work on to increase their overall strength for that lift. Failure helps us to learn and then get better from it.

This is the same in every part of your life. You should be excited for failure, since it will help you learn and grow! After every failure, we want to reflect on what happened and analyze it so we can pick out those pieces that need to be adjusted, to make it better the next round.

We expect them to fail. That's the only way to discover their true strength. Without failure, we never find our limits—or break through them. The same applies to life. The most successful people in history failed repeatedly before achieving greatness. The difference? They saw failure as feedback, not defeat.

Somewhere along the line of your faith journey, you have seen yourself as a failure to God because you are not "good enough." Well, none of us are good enough. We fail all the time. We always sin. We are imperfect, we are human.

The only human in history that was ever perfect and never failed was Jesus Christ, and we are not Him, so stop trying to be perfect. Jesus died for our sins and our failures so that we may be perfect in Him. There is nothing we can do to earn the grace of God, it has been given as a gift to us!

> *"For by grace you have been saved through faith.*
> *And this is not your own doing; it is the gift of God,*
> *not a result of works, so that no one may boast. For*
> *we are his workmanship, created in Christ Jesus for*
> *good works, which God prepared beforehand, that we*
> *should walk in them." —Ephesians 2:8-10 (ESV)*

You must take those failures and learn from them, because God uses all things for good, so don't let it hold you back, use it to become extraordinary!

The most successful people in the world used this to become extraordinary. The greatest businesses, the greatest inventions, and all the amazing advances in our world happened due to people not letting failure stop them. They had it lead them and guide them to their amazing result!

Most don't ever look at the journey it took someone to get to that end result, they just see the positive result, get jealous, and say things along the lines of that they are really lucky, must be a trust fund baby, they must have great genetics, and blah blah blah. Nope, they had grit and discipline and grew from their failures.

I see this so often in health. People comparing themselves to other people and because they are not where the 'healthy' person is in their journey, they sort of shun them and say that they must have good genes and make other excuses of why that person is able to do it, and they do it without knowing the person nor the journey they have been through. They don't see the amount of time, effort, energy, and failures that went into getting the results they now see. People make assumptions about the person that is filled with joy and peace in their life, but don't realize that they have gone through hell and back to have that joy and peace, and it has helped them develop an amazing relationship with Christ. They are farther along in their journey and have gone through a lot to get there, but that doesn't mean that you can't get there too.

To get farther along the journey, you have to keep going. You can't just stop, or you will never reach that destination, whatever that may be for you; financial freedom, the career you are dreaming of, a healthier and fit life, or a relationship with Jesus. Just because it didn't work yet, does not mean it won't work, you just have to keep at it!

"I fear not the man who has practiced 10,000 kicks once, but I fear the man who has practiced one kick 10,000 times." - Bruce Lee

This quote reminds us that success doesn't come from trying a hundred things one time. It comes from staying committed to one thing long enough to master it. Consistency beats novelty. It's not about how many different paths you attempt—it's about staying on the right path long enough to see it through.

Doing random different things is not how you become successful, it is staying focused and persistent, through obstacles and failures, that will make you successful. Choose the path of resistance, take on the fear of failure and overcome that mindset to become the extraordinary you.

Overcoming the Fear of Failure

The fear of failure can paralyze you, keeping you from stepping into your extraordinary life. However, failure is not the end—it's a part of growth and learning.

Reframing Failure

- **Failure is Feedback**: Each setback is an opportunity to learn and refine your approach.

- **God's Perspective on Failure**: God uses our mistakes to shape us into stronger, wiser individuals. Romans 8:28 reminds us that "in all things, God works for the good of those who love Him."

- **The Only True Failure**: Failing to try is the only way to truly fail.

Reflection Questions: Overcoming What Holds You Back

- What fears are currently preventing you from pursuing your God-given purpose?

- How has fear of failure shaped your decisions in the past?

- How would your life change if you viewed failure as growth rather than defeat?

- How can trusting in God help you face challenges with confidence?

Habits to Overcome Fear of Failure

- **Redefine Success**: Focus on progress, not perfection. Celebrate small wins along the way.

- **Take Small Risks**: Step out of your comfort zone in manageable ways to build resilience and confidence.

- **Reflect on Past Successes**: Remind yourself of previous challenges you've overcome.

- **Shift Your Perspective**: Replace "What if I fail?" with "What if I succeed?"

- **Pray for Courage**: Ask God for strength to face challenges boldly and trust Him through the process.

Bringing It Together: Actions to Overcoming Fear

Overcoming the fear of failure is a huge step—but what comes next?

Many people think that once they get past fear, change will just happen. But real transformation—whether in fitness, faith, or any area of life—requires more than courage. It takes a clear understanding of where you are and what specific steps to take next to move forward.

This is where most people get stuck. They want change, but because they don't know what stage they're in, they either try to skip ahead too fast or give up when it feels hard.

So let me ask you:

- What's one small action you can take today to overcome your fear?
- What setback can you turn into your comeback?

Change is not a single event—it's a process. And if you understand the process, you can stop feeling lost and start making progress, one action step at a time.

Final Charge: Fear Is a Liar–Fail Forward

Your fear of failure is the chain holding you back from becoming the extraordinary you. But here's the truth: Failure is not the enemy—it's the teacher that sharpens you. You will stumble. You will fall. But when you rise again, you rise stronger, wiser, and more equipped for the mission God has placed on your life.

Don't let the fear of failing stop you from even trying. Don't let the "what ifs" hold you back from stepping forward. Remember, the only true failure is quitting. Every other setback is a setup for a greater comeback.

Will you choose fear—or will you choose faith? Will you let failure define you—or will you let it refine you?

This is your moment to decide: Will you stay stuck in fear, or will you step forward and grow stronger through every fall?

It's time to fail forward. It's time to rise. It's time to become the extraordinary version of you.

In the next chapter, I'm going to introduce you to a powerful framework that has helped countless people—both in fitness and in faith—successfully transform their lives. It's called The Transtheoretical Model of Behavior Change, and when you know where you are in this model, you can stop guessing and start growing into the extraordinary person God has called you to be.

The Transtheoretical Model of Behavior Change— A Path to Transformation in Fitness and Faith

After addressing fear of failure, it's critical to recognize that lasting transformation doesn't happen overnight. Even when you believe in your ability to change, there's still a process to follow. Change is not a one-time event—it's a journey that requires daily effort, small wins, and persistence through setbacks.

Unfortunately, this is where most people struggle. They want to jump straight from inspiration to transformation, but when results don't come fast, they give up. Or they skip necessary steps like preparing mentally and spiritually, and when obstacles arise, they crumble under pressure.

That's why understanding the stages of change is essential. When you know where you are in the process, you can take the right next step instead of trying to leap ahead—and that's how real, lasting change happens in both fitness and faith.

This is also a key part of The Extraordinary Strength Method™— helping you understand and embrace each stage so that you can build lasting transformation from the inside out.

The Five Stages of Change in Fitness and Faith

1. Precontemplation (Ignorance or Resistance)

- **Fitness Perspective**: At this stage, people do not recognize the need for change. They may believe exercise is unnecessary, claim they don't have time, or assume they are "too far gone" to improve their health.

- **Faith Perspective**: Spiritually, this is the phase where someone may feel disconnected from faith, indifferent to gratitude, or unaware of how spiritual growth could benefit their life.

- **Key to Progress**: Awareness. Exposure to new ideas, testimonies, and stories of transformation in others can spark curiosity and open the door to possibility.

I work with a man who we'll call Matt, a father of two who walked into my gym with his arms crossed, skeptical of everything. He had never prioritized his health and viewed fitness as something for "younger guys." It wasn't until his doctor warned him about his heart health that he even considered training. That was his wake-up call. At first, he resisted—every movement seemed like a chore, and he questioned why he was even there. But over time, he started seeing what his body was capable of. Awareness was the first step toward transformation.

2. Contemplation (Recognition and Interest)

- **Fitness Perspective**: Here, an individual acknowledges they need to exercise and eat better, but they are still weighing the pros and cons. Fear of failure or uncertainty about the process can cause hesitation.

- **Faith Perspective**: This is when someone begins to question their spiritual life. They may start exploring faith-based principles or consider how gratitude and God could bring meaning to their life—but they're unsure.

- **Key to Progress**: Education. Learning about the benefits of change and hearing others' success stories makes transformation seem possible.

I've seen this stage many times in my gym, but one story stands out. A woman named, let's call her Sarah, had struggled with weight her entire life. She wanted to change but was terrified of failing—she had tried and quit too many times before. It was the same with her faith; she wanted to trust in something bigger than herself but had too many doubts. She started reading about fitness, watching transformation stories, and doing the same with faith—listening to podcasts, reading scripture, and journaling. Over time, her hesitation turned into belief, and belief turned into action.

3. Preparation (Commitment to Change)

- **Fitness Perspective**: At this stage, people begin to prepare for action. They sign up for a gym, buy workout gear, or plan a schedule—but may not be fully consistent yet.

- **Faith Perspective**: This is when someone starts praying, attending church, or practicing daily gratitude—but these habits aren't yet fully integrated into their life.

- **Key to Progress**: Actionable plans. Small, manageable commitments—like a thirty-day fitness challenge or a daily gratitude journal—build momentum.

When I first committed to daily gratitude journaling, it felt forced—just another item on my checklist. But I started small: writing down one thing I was grateful for each morning before my workout. Within weeks, it shifted my mindset. I began to see opportunities where I once saw obstacles. Small steps create big shifts.

4. Action (Implementing New Habits)

- **Fitness Perspective**: Exercise and nutrition are now part of daily life. The person trains consistently, eats better, and starts seeing results.

- **Faith Perspective**: Faith practices—like prayer, scripture, gratitude, and service—are becoming natural and daily.

- **Key to Progress**: Support. Coaches, partners, and accountability groups help sustain new habits.

One of my favorite transformations is a girl, let's call her Betty, who came to me with no prior fitness experience. She struggled through her first month, but I noticed something: every time she trained, she felt pride. She started waking up earlier, setting goals, and taking ownership of her health. Eventually, she became the one inspiring others in class. The same happens in faith—what starts as a discipline eventually becomes second nature, shaping who we are.

5. Maintenance (Sustaining Transformation)

- **Fitness Perspective**: The person has successfully integrated exercise and proper nutrition into their lifestyle, avoiding relapse into old habits.

- **Faith Perspective**: Faith and gratitude become ingrained in daily life, even in times of struggle. The person has built a resilient mindset that sustains them through challenges.

- **Key to Progress**: Consistency. Establishing rituals and resilient habits that adapt to life's obstacles ensures lasting change.

One of my proudest moments as a coach was seeing my brother, Christian, return to the gym after suffering an injury. He could have quit, but instead, he adapted—he trained differently, focused on recovery, and stayed connected. Similarly, in faith, real transformation isn't about never struggling; it's about staying the course when trials come. Christian had built resilience, both in body and in mindset. Real transformation isn't about never struggling—it's about staying in the fight.

Relapse and Recommitment—The Reality of the Journey

Change is not linear. Many people cycle through these stages multiple times. Relapse into old habits—whether skipping workouts, neglecting prayer, or falling into negativity—is normal. The key is recognizing setbacks not as failures but as opportunities to recommit.

"For the righteous falls seven times and rises again." — Proverbs 24:16 (NIV)

Both in fitness and faith, the real strength lies in getting back up, refining the approach, and moving forward again.

Reflection Questions: Applying TTM in Your Life

- Where am I on my fitness journey? Am I resisting change, contemplating it, or actively working toward it?
- How does my faith align with my personal growth? Am I nurturing it as intentionally as I train my body?
- What support systems can I create to maintain momentum in both areas?

Bring It Together: Habits and Actions for Behavior Change

Daily or weekly behaviors to build momentum at each stage of change.

Precontemplation – Ignorance or Resistance

- Read or listen to 1 transformation story per week
- Reflect weekly: "What if I'm wrong about what's possible for me?"

Contemplation – Recognition and Interest

- Journal 3 reasons why you want to change
- Spend 5 minutes daily in quiet reflection or prayer

Preparation – Committing to Change

- Set a weekly plan (ex: 2 workouts, 2 spiritual practices)
- Start a gratitude or habit tracker

Action – Implementing New Habits

- Log fitness and faith habits daily
- Begin your day with 3 minutes of prayer or intention-setting

Maintenance – Sustaining Transformation

- Maintain 1 weekly ritual (meal prep, devotional, journaling)
- Identify personal "red flags" of relapse and rehearse your response

Relapse – Reset & Recommit

- Use a 3-day reset: workout, prayer, journaling
- Keep Proverbs 24:16 (ESV) visible: "*Though the righteous fall seven times and rises again.*"

Final Charge: The Path to Becoming Extraordinary

Transformation is a lifelong process of growth, grace, and persistence. Whether you're working on a stronger body, deeper faith, or a sharper mind, you don't have to do it all at once—and you don't have to do it alone. And that's exactly what The Extraordinary Strength Method™ is designed to help you do—guide you through every stage of change so that you keep moving forward even when life gets hard.

So wherever you are in the process—whether you're just thinking about change, taking your first steps, or maintaining a lifestyle—keep going. Every small step brings you closer to the extraordinary version of yourself God designed you to be.

The key is to keep moving forward, one step at a time. And as we'll see in the next chapter, your ability to take ownership and keep going—especially when it's hard—will unlock your extraordinary strength.

Pillar 3: Responsibility

Taking Ownership of Your Life

If you want to become the extraordinary version of yourself, there's a mindset you must develop—the mindset of responsibility.

You've already worked through belief, facing fear, and understanding the process of change. But here's a truth that few people want to admit: No real transformation happens without ownership.

Some things that happen in life may not be your fault. But how you respond to them is your responsibility.

Galatians 6:5 (ESV) reminds us, *"For each will have to bear his own load."*

We all carry burdens. Some are unfair, some are tragic—but only you can choose whether to stay stuck or to rise up and move forward.

The Story of Radical Responsibility: Brandon's Journey

To understand what radical responsibility looks like, let me share the story of one of the most inspiring men I know—Brandon Person.

On any given day, if you walk into Erie Fitness Academy, you will likely find Brandon Person working with a client or coaching a class, singing and dancing, and making everyone's time there enjoyable. His upbeat demeanor and character fills others with joy, while his encouragement and inspiration will make you want to give your all in all you do. He is a Coach and Operations Manager at Erie Fitness Academy. His story is inspiring on so many levels, much due to the pure grit and determination this man has. By looking at Brandon, you would not know what he has been through. He is a master of turning obstacles into opportunities. Due to his obstacles, he is able to inspire and help so many people take on their obstacles and take responsibility for their lives. We are blessed to have him on our team, and I love watching him grow, while helping others change their lives as well. It is actually a blessing that he is still alive.

On October 23rd, 2020, we had just hired him, and he was on his way to pick up his final check from his previous job. He was riding his motorcycle on a two-lane one-way street when the truck beside him ran into him and threw him off his bike and pinned him underneath a parked car. He ended up with a concussion, broken left scapula, eleven broken ribs, one punctured lung, the other lung collapsed, two broken lumbar vertebrae, a heart contusion, a hematoma in his left hip, and a compound fracture of his left leg. They were going to cut off his left leg but as the doctor was getting his tools out for the amputation, he pulled up the covers that were over Brandon's body and saw that he was in fantastic shape. He decided to give Brandon a chance and worked for endless hours putting his leg back together. They told him he may not ever walk again without a cane, let alone lift and workout like he did. Brandon was in the best shape of his life before that accident. He not only almost lost his leg, he almost lost his life. He had a choice now: to let his circumstances define him for the rest of his life, or take responsibility. Can you guess the route and mindset he took?

Most people would have accepted that fate. But Brandon chose a different path—the path of ownership.

He refused to let his accident define him. He didn't make excuses. Instead, he fought back with discipline, courage, and faith.

Today, Brandon is stronger than ever:

- Deadlift: 589 pounds
- Squat: 501 pounds
- Bench Press: 325 pounds
- Placed 3rd in a powerlifting meet
- Placed 1st in the Arnold Classic

From not being able to walk, to becoming stronger than he was before—Brandon's story is living proof that when you take responsibility for your life, you become unstoppable.

His choice to take responsibility not only greatly impacted his future, but the future of his daughter, our business, and all those he has contact with now and throughout the rest of his life. The ripple effect from his choice to take responsibility is positively impacting so many lives, and I cannot even imagine how far that ripple will go.

"Blessed is the man who remains steadfast under trial, for when he has stood the test he will receive the crown of life, which God has promised to those who love him." —James 1:12 (ESV)

He was truly tested and is now blessing others because of his trials and his choice to take ownership of his life. His story is inspiring, and due to the pure grit and determination he has shown, he is able to inspire and help so many people take on their own obstacles and take responsibility for their lives.

Taking Responsibility: Your First Step to Extraordinary

Like Brandon, you have a choice: To stay stuck in your excuses, or to take ownership of your life and future. Nothing else in this book—no belief, no action step—will work if you refuse to take responsibility. That's why ownership is a foundational pillar of The Extraordinary Strength Method™.

Whether you've been dealt a tough hand, made mistakes, or faced setbacks, it's still on you to decide what happens next. No one is coming to save you. But you've been given the tools to rise—and God has equipped you to carry your load.

Later on, we will talk about the Parable of the Talents and the story of the three builders—one of the clearest examples of responsibility and purpose. Whether you multiply what God has given you—or bury it—depends on your willingness to take ownership. Don't look for excuses for your life, take that ownership, and then you can start moving onward and forward!

Reflection Questions: Taking Ownership of Your Life

- Where in your life are you making excuses? What excuses have you been making that are holding you back?

- What areas of your health, faith, or relationships need improvement?

- How can you take better ownership of your health, mindset, and faith journey?

- How can you take responsibility for your current situation and start moving forward?

- What does living with responsibility for your God-given purpose look like in action?

- How will you hold yourself accountable for your growth moving forward?

Habits to Build Ownership

- Self-Awareness: Spend 5–10 minutes each day reflecting on your actions and choices.

- Set Intentional Goals: Identify specific, purpose-driven goals in your faith, fitness, or personal life.

- Stop Complaining: Challenge yourself to go one day at a time without blaming others or external factors

Bringing It Together: Responsibility In Action

Commit to Radical Responsibility

- Write down one area of your life where you've been making excuses. Today, choose to take ownership—no matter how difficult it feels. Pray for strength, and then act.

Shift from Excuses to Action

- Each time you catch yourself blaming circumstances or others, pause and reframe the situation:

    - What can you do to change or improve it?

    - What's one action step you can take right now?

Start Your Day with a Responsibility Reset

- Each morning, ask yourself:

    - What am I responsible for today?

    - Who will be impacted by the choices I make?

- Write down your answers as a reminder to take ownership from the start of the day.

End Your Day with an Accountability Check

- Reflect in your journal:

    - Did I take responsibility for my actions today?

    - Where did I let excuses creep in?

    - How will I do better tomorrow?

Take the Next Bold Step

- Don't just read and reflect—move. Identify one action you've been avoiding because of fear or blame, and take the first step toward it within the next twentyfour hours.

- Example: If you've avoided a difficult conversation, schedule it. If you've neglected your health, plan your next workout or meal prep session.

Serve Others Through Your Example

- Responsibility is contagious. Share your story, encourage someone else, or offer support to a friend or family member who needs it. Let your life inspire others to take ownership of their own.

Final Charge: Own It or Stay Stuck

If you want to live an extraordinary life—if you want to fulfill the purpose God has for you—you must take full responsibility.

No more excuses. No more waiting for life to get easier. Own your life. Own your mindset. Own your purpose.

Responsibility is the first step toward becoming the person God designed you to be—and it's the foundation that holds everything else together in The Extraordinary Strength Method™.

So, I ask you, are you ready to take ownership of your life and step into the extraordinary?

Taking responsibility is the first step to becoming the extraordinary version of yourself, but it's not enough on its own. Once you've taken ownership of your life and choices, you need to know what you're building your life on.

What do you truly stand for? What are the non-negotiable standards that will guide your actions when life gets hard?

If you don't define your core values, the world will define them for you—and you'll be swayed by whatever is easiest, most comfortable, or most popular. Taking ownership means choosing to live by a higher standard—one that aligns with who God says you are and the purpose He's placed on your life.

In the next chapter, we'll dive into how to define your core values and set life standards that will keep you focused, grounded, and growing—so you can keep moving toward the extraordinary life God has called you to live.

Pillar 4: Values and Standards

Foundations of the Extraordinary—Building Unshakable Values and Standards

What do you stand for—truly? If someone looked at your actions, not your words, would they know?

Most people have never taken the time to define their values. They think they know what they believe in, but when life gets hard, they crumble because they have no foundation. If you don't define what you stand for now, life's challenges will define it for you—and you may not like where that leads.

I learned this lesson firsthand.

When I was at my level 1 certification for Training for Warriors, Martin Rooney asked us a powerful question: "What are your core values—what do you believe in so strongly that you would die for them?"

I was stunned. Sure, I had things I valued—family, faith, fitness—but had I ever stood behind them with everything in me? Had I ever truly defined them? The truth was, I hadn't. Like most people, I wrote down something generic just to answer the question. But that question stuck with me. And it forced me to realize: If I didn't define my values, I would never live them.

Today, I know my values, and because of that, decisions are easier. I have direction. I know who I am. And that's what I want for you.

Developing a set of core values is not a one night ordeal, it takes dedicated time. But now that I have my core values, decisions in life are much easier since I always have direction in which way I should go.

What Are Values?

Values are "a person's principles or standards of behavior; one's judgment of what is important in life." Ah, standards of behavior. That is essential here. The way you conduct yourself is based on your core values! And here's the truth most people don't realize: Your values aren't what you say—they're what you live.

Show me your actions, and I'll show you your real values.

If you say you value health but never train or eat well, you don't value health.

If you say you value family but are glued to your phone when you're with them, you don't value family.

If you say you value faith but spend no time with God or serving others, that's not a value—it's lip service.

Values are shown in behavior. They are your personal code of conduct—how you operate in every area of life.

Our moral compass is from God, but without the right core values in place and acted upon daily, our moral compass can easily be swayed by others. Romans 12:2 (ESV) says, *"Do not be conformed to this world, but be transformed by the renewal of your mind, that by testing you may discern what is the will of God, what is good and acceptable and perfect."* God does not want you to follow the crowd, He wants you to follow Him! The mindset required to live out your God-given purpose has to have values to act upon and follow, or you will fall prey to things of this world and not be able to discern God's will for you.

> *"If you don't stand for something, you'll fall for anything." - Alexander Hamilton*

This isn't just a clever phrase—it's a warning. When you lack firm convictions, you become easy prey for the shifting winds of culture, peer pressure, and empty promises. You'll find yourself standing for what's popular, not for what's true. And when the world's applause fades, you'll realize you were never standing at all.

We see this everywhere today. Constant division, people going to extremes, and others blindly following crowds simply because they're afraid to stand alone. Many only stand their ground when there are no consequences, or because they're surrounded by others doing the same. That's not conviction. That's conformity. And it leaves people lost, without a true direction or purpose.

But you are called to something greater. Let your values be forged in the fire of faith, grounded in Scripture, and strengthened through discipline—so that when the world pushes, you stand firm in God's truth.

Following the crowd rarely leads to good. Matthew 7:13-14 (ESV) says, "*Enter through the narrow gate. For wide is the gate and broad is the road that leads to destruction, and many enter through it. But small is the gate and narrow the road that leads to life, and only a few find it.*"

You need to set your own core values, that way when challenges in life come up, you have direction on what to do, not just follow what the world is doing.

The World is Lowering the Standard – But You Can't

Values are 'standards of behavior,' so that means the core values we set for ourselves are the standards and expectations we set for ourselves, and we need to set our standards high. Society has done a great job at lowering the bar for just about everything in life.

Let's be honest: Society's standards are painfully low.

- Schools have low expectations.
- Employees cut corners.
- Health standards are at an all-time low.
- Courtesy, respect, and kindness are disappearing.

Why? Because low standards are easy. But easy doesn't make you extraordinary.

God has high standards, and though we will always fall short, that doesn't mean we stop striving. Living by high standards is the path to strength, character, and purpose. If you don't define what you stand for, the world will define it for you—and it will be whatever is easiest, not what's right.

There is work that has to be done. People have to be challenged, disciplined, and have consequences if those standards are not met. It doesn't matter what is preached, what matters is what is tolerated. The standard will always be set at what is tolerated, even if someone preaches a higher standard.

As we will talk about, it creates discomfort when standards are set high. People do not do well with discomfort. So the easy route is the one we take.

God has standards set for all, and they are high. They are so high, we cannot hit them. We always fall short. But, by the grace of God, we were given Jesus. Though we have been saved through faith in Him, that does not mean we stop trying to hit those standards. Living out a Christian life means doing our best each day to live as Jesus lived. To follow those standards to the best of our ability, not to turn a blind eye to them because "we are forgiven."

It is not an easy road. Hitting standards in today's world is easy. Literally anyone can do it. It is easy to be average. You don't want to be average, though. You want to be extraordinary. You want to have purpose and meaning to your life.

Set those standards high. If you fall a bit short sometimes, that is okay. You are still making greater progress than if you set your standards low and hit them every single time.

Your values should have the highest standards of anything in your life, since they will dictate all the actions of your life. If you hold yourself to the highest standard and values, you will succeed at anything and everything in your life. But, if you tolerate poor actions and allow yourself to stray from your values, you will fall back in with the crowd and stay average, just like everyone else.

Values Require Sacrifice

Values are a transaction. When you value something, you are always going to have to sacrifice something; time, effort, energy, money, short-term gratification, etc. The transaction is always worth it with something truly valuable, though. If you have high standards of values, you will never get "buyer's remorse" with your actions and decisions since it will always yield the higher reward in the end, even if you had to sacrifice something that would have given you instant gratification at the time. The delayed gratification is always greater.

It will not be easy, it is not comfortable, but it will be worth it. It will take discipline and discomfort to find those core values and to follow through with them. But once you have them in place and act on them every single day, you will be closer to that extraordinary you and will fulfill your purpose.

Reflection Questions: Living Out Your Values

- What are the non-negotiable values you are committed to living by, no matter what?

- Where in your life have you compromised your values or allowed the world to set your standards?

- How do your current actions reflect (or not reflect) the values you claim to hold?

- What would it look like to raise your standards in your faith, fitness, relationships, and work?

- Are you willing to make sacrifices—time, effort, comfort—to live out your values daily?

- When life gets hard, what core values will keep you grounded in your God-given purpose?

- How will you hold yourself accountable when you're tempted to take the easy way out?

- What does it mean to you to "enter through the narrow gate" in your life right now?

Habits to Build Values and Standards

- Scripture Alignment: Pick one scripture each week that reinforces your values and meditate on it daily (e.g., Romans 12:2, Matthew 7:13-14).

- Define Your Core Values: Write out your top 3–5 core values and keep them visible in your daily life (journal, phone background, mirror).

- Live It Out Challenge: Each day, intentionally act in alignment with one core value—track it in your journal.

- Discomfort Practice: Do one thing each week that pushes you outside your comfort zone in pursuit of your values (e.g., having a hard conversation, standing up for your beliefs, sacrificing comfort for growth).

- Gratitude for Values: At the end of each day, write down one way you honored your values—and one area for improvement.

Bringing It Together: How to Build Unshakable Values and Standards

- Clarify What You Stand For: What do you believe so strongly that you would stand for it even when no one else does?

- Align Actions with Beliefs: Check where your behavior doesn't match what you say you value—and adjust.

- Raise Your Standards: Set higher expectations for yourself than the world does.

- Be Ready to Pay the Price: Know what sacrifices living by your values will require—and make them.

- Anchor in God's Word: Base your values on God's truth, not shifting culture.

Final Charge: What Do You Stand For?

If you want to become the extraordinary version of yourself, you have to know what you stand for and live it—even when it's hard. Reminder of Matthew 7:13-14 (ESV), "*Enter through the narrow gate. For wide is the gate and broad is the road that leads to destruction, and many enter through it. But small is the gate and narrow the road that leads to life, and only a few find it.*"

The Extraordinary Strength Method™ will help you define and live by your values with unwavering standards—so when life gets hard, you stay aligned with your purpose.

But today, I want to challenge you to start:

- What do you stand for?
- What are the non-negotiable values that will guide you?
- What are you willing to sacrifice to live those out?

Extraordinary people don't follow the crowd—they live by unshakable values and standards. So what do you choose?

Defining your values and raising your standards is essential, but let's be real, knowing what you stand for is only the beginning. It's one thing to write down what you value. It's an entirely different thing to live those values every single day, especially when life gets uncomfortable.

The truth is, you will be tested. There will be days when you don't feel like showing up, when it would be easier to lower your standards, make excuses, and take the path of least resistance.

And that's why discipline is the game-changer. Discipline is what turns good intentions into real transformation. Discipline is what allows you to stay aligned with your values when everything in you wants to quit.

Discipline and discomfort are the secret weapons of extraordinary people—the ones who don't just say what they value, but live it out boldly in every part of their lives.

In the next chapter, we're going to dive into what discipline really looks like—why motivation isn't enough, why embracing discomfort is essential, and how to develop the kind of discipline that will carry you through every challenge on the path to becoming the extraordinary you.

Pillar 5: Discipline and Discomfort

The Path of Resistance—Discipline, Discomfort, and the Road to Extraordinary

If you're serious about becoming the extraordinary version of yourself—the person God created you to be—there's one thing you absolutely need to understand: Nothing great is built without discipline.

It doesn't matter how clear your values are or how high you've set your standards, without discipline, those values will collapse the moment life gets hard. Discipline is what makes everything else work.

The problem is, most people are waiting for motivation to carry them through. They think that if they "feel like it" they'll act right. But here's a truth that may hit you hard: Motivation will fail you.

Motivation is a feeling—discipline is a decision.

Motivation is what you feel when everything is easy. Discipline is what you do when everything gets hard.

Motivation fades. Discipline carries you through.

Discipline is what keeps you living out your values when no one is watching and when every part of you wants to quit.

If motivation was enough, we wouldn't have an obesity epidemic, an epidemic of failing faith, or a society drowning in laziness and excuses. Motivation doesn't get you out of bed at 4:30 a.m. to train. Motivation doesn't say no to fast food. Motivation doesn't get you to pick up your Bible when you're exhausted.

Discipline does.

But here's the kicker: Discipline doesn't happen without discomfort.

Discipline doesn't happen without discomfort. If you want to fulfill your purpose and become the extraordinary person God created, you must, as Martin Rooney says, 'get comfortable being uncomfortable.' Discipline and the ability to embrace discomfort are the twin skills that make anyone extraordinary—and they're both built, not born.

We live in a world that runs from discomfort at all costs—always looking for the easy way out, the shortcut, the path of least resistance. But you need to understand this: The path of least resistance never leads to greatness—only the path of resistance does.

If you want to live a life of purpose, if you want to become extraordinary, you have to train yourself to get comfortable being uncomfortable. Discipline and discomfort are the crucibles where strength is built, faith is refined, and purpose comes to life.

In this chapter, we're going to dive into:

- Why motivation won't get you where you want to go.

- What discipline actually looks like in real life.

- How embracing discomfort will give you the strength to live out your purpose.

- And how this ties into The Extraordinary Strength Method™—because without discipline, nothing else in this book will stick.

So let me ask you this before we dive in: What's the dream God has placed on your heart that you've been too uncomfortable to pursue?

Because by the end of this chapter, you'll know exactly how to develop the strength to go after it—no matter how uncomfortable it gets.

Why Motivation Will Never Be Enough

I am sure you have heard others say motivation is greater than discipline before, but let me dig into this. Most people seek motivation for any area in their life they want to make a right change in, whether it's their health, faith, finances, career, relationships, or anything else. They are searching for something within their mind that gives them a "I want to go do this" attitude. Though you can sometimes find that, it will not be there often and especially when you need it most.

Motivation is fleeting and weak. It cannot stand up to excuses, challenges, or discomfort of any kind. If motivation could truly be used all the time, we would not have an obesity epidemic, people falling from faith, or an entitled lazy society.

Motivation is "the general desire to do something." Even the definition is lackluster. General desire?! Can you see why just having a 'general desire to do something' won't help you become extraordinary?

It has to go deeper than just a desire, it has to hit home! It has to be emotional and purpose-driven or else it won't happen. Motivation doesn't get someone up at 4:30 a.m. to go train 3-5 days per week. Motivation doesn't keep someone eating the right food and not stopping at fast food multiple times per week. Motivation doesn't get someone to sit down and read their bible every day. Motivation doesn't get someone to have conversations with God all throughout the day asking for guidance and discernment in every area of their life, giving thanksgiving no matter the circumstance, and praying for everyone, not just themselves. Motivation doesn't get a person to change their habits and way of life to become extraordinary.

This is where discipline comes in.

What Real Discipline Looks Like

Discipline is defined as "to train oneself to do something in a controlled and habitual way." This means discipline is more than just a mindset, it is a mental skill. That means it can be learned and trained by any person. Habits and skills are built over time by repeating those same actions consistently. It doesn't just happen, it takes time, effort, and energy. When you are training for something, like an event or a sport, there is a much bigger goal in mind than the excuses of not doing what is necessary to achieve that goal. You don't skip practices just because you don't "feel like it" at the time, because you know the result you want.

> *"Discipline is the ability to make yourself do something you don't want to do in order to get the result you really want to get" - Andy Andrews.*

No one is born inherently disciplined, it is a skill developed over time through discomfort to achieve a purpose greater than the excuses.

Embracing Discomfort as Training for Growth

Discomfort is what makes most people quit. But if you want to live an extraordinary life, you must train yourself to work with discomfort instead of running from it.

Discomfort is defined as "a state of unease, worry, or embarrassment." Discomfort is what makes most people fall off course or not even get on the course in the first place. The worry and fear of the 'what ifs' take hold and render us useless, making us go nowhere in life. But what if you didn't let it throw you off? What if you leaned into that discomfort and got from it, not just through it?

> "But God disciplines us for our good, in order that we may share in his holiness. No discipline seems pleasant at the time, but painful. Later on, however, it produces a harvest of righteousness and peace for those who have been trained by it. Therefore, strengthen your feeble arms and weak knees." - Hebrews 12:10b-13 (NLT)

As stated before, discipline happens through discomfort. It does not seem pleasant at the time, but it leads to greatness! A person's level of discomfort is going to vary based on the experiences they've had in their lives. Less discomfort in their life equals less ability to deal with discomfort later in their lives.

As Michael Easter talks about in his amazing book Comfort Crisis, "We are living progressively sheltered, sterile, temperature-controlled, overfed, underchallenged, safety-netted lives."

We live in an overly comfortable society, where things that are challenging and uncomfortable are being avoided at all cost. Think about it, we complain if it's hot outside and find places that have AC. We complain when it's cold outside and find a place cozy and warm.

People are choosing to not do their job well, called quiet quitting, so they don't engage in the uncomfortable conversation about quitting.

We have a society that is over 73 percent overweight and obese because working out and eating healthy is harder than sitting around and putting trash in their mouths, so they look for the easier way—like a pill or a surgery—to fix it for them.

People are abandoning their faith because things in their life became hard, and they can't handle the hard conversations with a non-believer.

Divorce, mental illness, depression and anxiety are at an all-time high. Preventable diseases are at an all-time high. Absolutely crazy.

Then Michael also states, *"But a radical new body of evidence shows that people are at their best—physically harder, mentally tougher, and spiritually sounder—after experiencing the same discomforts our early ancestors were exposed to everyday. Scientists are finding that certain discomforts protect us from physical and psychological problems like obesity, heart disease, cancers, diabetes, depression, and anxiety, and even more fundamental issues like feeling a lack of meaning and purpose."*

Your ability to work with discomfort can change your entire life. If you want to become that extraordinary you and live out your purpose, discipline and discomfort are absolutes that need to be a part of your mental skill set.

This is one of my favorite things about working out and training; it is all about building a higher ability to deal with discomfort, and it works for any person, no matter where they are at in their health journey. In the very beginning, just going through the door takes courage and discipline. Then taking on the discomfort of going through a workout, even if it's for fifteen minutes, is still a great step out of the comfort zone, and you'd be so glad you went in and did it. There is satisfaction felt in the accomplishment. Well, now that your comfort zone just got a tiny bit bigger, tomorrow will be just a bit easier to get in through those doors and complete a workout.

Now, the building blocks of change and transformation start to happen. Stacking two, three, or even four days of training per week throughout the month: Now that discipline is growing, the comfort zone is expanding.

The same parallels with your faith. You don't go to church or read your bible regularly. There is discomfort in walking through the doors of a church, and it's holding you back from going. It takes courage and discipline to make it back through those doors. But once you do, you'd be glad you went and there'd be satisfaction and peace felt. This helps you to open His word more, and it becomes easier. Little efforts compound.

You are training for life and have a bigger goal and purpose in mind. Building that discipline has to start with those small actions and remembering why you are doing it. Your why and purpose has to be bigger than your excuses, but once that discipline is built, you will be making great progress toward that purpose and will become the extraordinary you!

Training for Life

Here is the tricky part, the discomfort in the training of your life has to keep happening, though. Once something starts to become comfortable, change and progression forward will stop. You have to constantly be pushing into that discomfort and out of the comfort zone. Your comfort zone has grown, so your margin of error starts to decrease. Those right action steps need to keep happening. You have to keep increasing your weights, increasing the intensity in your metabolic training, and increasing the time and intentionality in God's word and time spent with Him throughout the day. Comfort leads to complacency, and there is no growth there. Often, you have to evaluate your training for your life and see where you are too comfortable and start pushing into that discomfort to become that extraordinary you and fulfill your purpose!

> *"Do you not know that in a race, all the runners run, but only one receives the prize? So run that you may obtain it. Every athlete exercises self-control in all things. They do it to receive a perishable wreath, but we are imperishable... But I discipline my body and keep it under control, lest after preaching to others I myself should be disqualified."*
> *- 1 Corinthians 9:24-25,27 (ESV)*

Paul speaks of athletes and their self-control and relates it to himself and keeping himself under control. This is discipline in practice. Athletes have very little to no margin of error. They must be completely disciplined, or they will not be able to compete with the others. If they decide to not workout because they don't 'feel like it,' or decide to eat trash food that day because they had a hard day, they would not succeed.

Top athletes in the world are paid millions of dollars because of their discipline and self-control. They did not get to the top due to genetics alone. Sure, it has some part to play, but there are many more in the world that have the right genes to play at the top level, but it is those that have disciplined themselves to their dream and purpose that made it to the top. They worked past their discomforts and challenges and got from them to become extraordinary.

This is possible for you and every person in the world. Everyone is running the race, but only those that have self-control and discipline are the ones that win the prize. This does not mean you have to be a high level athlete, but for you to fulfill your God-given purpose, you have to discipline yourself so you may obtain that prize! Don't let your self-limiting beliefs and challenges in life stop you, for if you overcome them, that is when the extraordinary breaks through.

Now what do you do when the challenge in life happens? What do you do when the trial happens?

Well, that is what you built your discipline for. The challenge is leading you to greater opportunity.

The more you have leaned into that discomfort while building your discipline, the easier it will be to put your head down and keep moving forward into the challenge.

> *"Consider it pure joy, my brothers and sisters, whenever*
> *you face trials of many kinds, because you know that*
> *the testing of your faith produces perseverance. Let*
> *perseverance finish its work so that you may be mature and*
> *complete, not lacking anything." - James 1:2-4 (NIV)*

These trials, challenges, obstacles, and discomforts lead to greater perseverance and the extraordinary you, as James says, 'mature and complete, not lacking anything.' Every time we face trials and get from them, we become better versions of ourselves.

This also leads to seeing things that used to be uncomfortable and challenging before as easy. The discomfort has become comfortable. The experiences in your life have now given you a greater tolerance for discomfort.

It is always crazy to look back at life and see the things we used to think were hard beforehand. Being able to look back and see that what used to be your initial goal in a workout is now part of your warmup. Looking back and seeing old notes you wrote for yourself during your bible study and seeing how far you have come in your relationship with Jesus.

Discipline, though often perceived as restrictive or burdensome, is the path to true freedom and fulfillment. When you commit to discipline, you are no longer a slave to fleeting emotions, distractions, or unhealthy habits. Instead, you take control of your life, aligning your actions with your purpose. This alignment fosters a sense of inner peace and confidence, as every disciplined choice moves you closer to becoming the person God designed you to be.

In fitness, discipline allows your body to grow stronger, more resilient, and capable of overcoming physical challenges you once thought impossible. The workouts that once felt overwhelming become empowering, and you realize the limits you believed you had were never real. The same principle applies to your mind. As you consistently discipline your thoughts, replacing negativity with truth and gratitude, you'll begin to experience clarity, peace, and joy. Mental discipline frees you from fear, doubt, and the lies that have kept you stuck. It allows you to take on life's challenges with a renewed sense of hope and confidence.

Spiritually, discipline connects you more deeply with God. Regular prayer, scripture study, and worship create a foundation for unshakable faith. This consistency builds spiritual strength, helping you face adversity with trust and courage. When you make time for God daily, you'll discover how His guidance shapes your decisions, aligns your priorities, and fills your heart with purpose. What once felt like an obligation transforms into a deep well of joy and fulfillment, as you grow closer to Him.

The beauty of discipline is how it transforms over time. What begins as difficult, small steps in discomfort turns into freedom and strength in body, mind, and spirit. Every act of discipline compounds, creating a ripple effect in your life. As you grow stronger, you'll find that the things you once struggled with now empower you, and the life you once dreamed of is within reach. Through discipline, you discover that fulfillment isn't found in comfort or ease—it's found in the freedom to fully live out your purpose with confidence, strength, and joy. Discipline and discomfort will be key in fulfilling your purpose and becoming the extraordinary you!

The Key: Discipline and Discomfort

Discipline is the cornerstone of success in all areas of life. It is the ability to do what needs to be done, even when you don't feel like it. Discipline is built through repeated action and refined in the crucible of discomfort.

Discomfort is where growth happens. While our society avoids discomfort, leaning into it builds resilience, strength, and purpose. Growth requires stepping outside your comfort zone regularly.

Motivation vs. Discipline

- Are you waiting for motivation to act?
- What systems can you build to act without needing motivation?

Discomfort as Growth

- When have you grown most—during comfort or discomfort?
- What discomfort could God be using to shape you right now?

Discipline for Freedom and Fulfillment

- How disciplined are you daily in faith, fitness, and mindset?
- How can small daily wins make you stronger?

Habits to Build Discipline and Embrace Discomfort

Daily Habits:

- Morning Momentum: Wake up at the same time daily. Start with prayer, reflection, or challenging physical activity.
- Daily Non-Negotiables: Pick 1–3 critical actions (workout, Bible study, hard conversations) and get them done—no excuses.
- Gratitude and Reflection: End the day by journaling one moment of discomfort you overcame and one thing you're grateful for.

Weekly Habits:

- Plan and Progress: Set specific faith and fitness goals (e.g., attend church, complete workouts).

- Stretch Your Comfort Zone: Choose one thing each week that makes you uncomfortable—fasting, intense workouts, or serving in new ways.

- Accountability Check-In: Share progress with a trusted friend or mentor.

Bringing It Together: Action Steps to Build Discipline & Embrace Discomfort

- Define Your Non-Negotiables

  - Write down 1–3 daily non-negotiables—actions you will commit to every day, no matter what. Examples: a workout, Bible study, or prayer time.

- Choose Your Discomfort Challenge

  - Each week, intentionally step into one area of discomfort—whether it's a cold shower, a hard conversation, or pushing through a tough workout. Let discomfort be your training ground.

- Replace Motivation with Systems

  - Design simple systems that make discipline automatic—set alarms, block time in your calendar, prep meals in advance. Don't rely on motivation—make it easy to stay consistent.

- Celebrate Wins & Learn from Losses

- At the end of each day, journal one moment where you overcame discomfort and one area where you need to improve. Let both wins and losses fuel your growth.

- Anchor Your Why in Scripture

  - Meditate daily on verses that reinforce discipline, like Hebrews 12:11 or 1 Corinthians 9:24-27. Let God's Word shape your perspective on discomfort.

- Build Your Discipline Muscle

  - Start small. Pick one area to focus on—like waking up earlier, sticking to a workout, or reading Scripture daily. Then build on that momentum each week.

- Accountability Matters

  - Find an accountability partner—someone who will challenge you to stay disciplined, not just when it's easy, but especially when it's hard.

- Commit to the Long Game

  - Write down your long-term vision—why discipline and discomfort matter to your purpose. Revisit this regularly to remind yourself of the bigger picture.

Discipline and discomfort are essential pillars of The Extraordinary Strength Method™. Without them, you cannot sustain the responsibility, values, or purpose that we've already explored. Through discipline, you move from merely wishing for a better life to building it—brick by brick, rep by rep.

Discipline frees you to live with strength, confidence, and purpose, even when life gets tough. And discomfort? Discomfort becomes your training ground for greatness.

The extraordinary life is on the other side of discipline. It's time to take that first uncomfortable step.

But discipline is only one side of the coin. To truly become extraordinary, you also need a mindset that shifts your focus from what you lack to what you have. In the next chapter, we're going to explore a powerful force that multiplies discipline and keeps you grounded through the process: Gratitude.

Let's discover how an attitude of gratitude can transform not only your discipline but your entire life.

Pillar 6: Gratitude

The Attitude that Fuels the Extraordinary

If discipline is the engine that drives you forward, gratitude is the fuel that keeps you going when the road gets tough.

Without gratitude, discipline becomes exhausting. But when gratitude fills your heart, discipline becomes worship, and discomfort becomes growth. Gratitude is what keeps you anchored to God's goodness when life feels overwhelming. It is a mindset that shifts your focus from what you lack to what you've been given. And when you begin to see your life as a gift, everything changes—your faith deepens, your health improves, your relationships strengthen, and your purpose becomes clearer.

Why Gratitude is the Fuel for Transformation

Gratitude has a profound impact on both faith and health. Yet, many people rarely practice it. Instead, most are consumed daily by stress, frustration, and what they lack. Shifting this mindset is life-changing—because gratitude can enhance your commitment, motivation, and overall well-being in every area. Without gratitude, discipline fades into burnout. But with gratitude, you endure longer, grow deeper, and stay aligned to your purpose.

"Give thanks in all circumstances; for this is the will of God in Christ Jesus for you." - 1 Thessalonians 5:18 (ESV)

Focusing on gratitude will make a massive change in anyone's life, including yours! Gratitude is not comparing yourself to others, it is reflecting and truly appreciating what you are blessed with in your life. It may feel awkward or difficult to begin practicing gratitude, but this simple shift in mindset will radically change your life. It will strengthen both your faith and fitness, nourishing your mind, body, and spirit.

Having an attitude of gratitude will impact your health through motivation and discipline, meaning that gratitude for one's physical abilities, no matter the level, can inspire consistent practice. When you recognize your body as a gift, you're more inclined to treat it well through exercise, balanced nutrition, and adequate rest. Those who practice gratitude are often more accepting of their bodies as they are, which can reduce self-criticism. This shift allows for a healthier approach to fitness and health, focused on well-being rather than comparison.

Focusing on gratitude during exercise can also make training and a healthy lifestyle more enjoyable, decreasing the likelihood of burnout. Instead of seeing workouts as a chore, if you practice gratitude, you are more likely to view them as opportunities for growth. When this shift is made, fitness and health becomes a natural part of your life, and your gratitude for your health will continue to grow, overflowing into all other areas of your life.

A grateful mindset also helps to promote recovery and resiliency. It improves recovery by reducing stress hormones and enhancing sleep quality, both of which are crucial for muscle repair and growth. It also builds resilience, helping you bounce back from setbacks, whether they're injuries or fitness plateaus.

Regularly expressing gratitude helps through life's setbacks and challenges as well. It helps you focus on positive aspects of your life and spiritual journey, reinforcing trust in God. When you acknowledge blessings, even in challenging times, it strengthens faith by fostering resilience and a sense of divine purpose, knowing that you are not going through this alone and there is a greater plan in motion, for He is always faithful.

Gratitude invites you to reflect on life's blessings, encouraging mindfulness and an awareness of the present moment and all the blessings you have received throughout your life. This awareness nurtures a deeper, more conscious faith, where you see life as an ongoing journey of grace and love.

Gratitude will help you with your relationships as well. Practicing gratitude often translates to a more compassionate and forgiving attitude, which will enhance relationships. Within communities, gratitude fosters unity and service, encouraging individuals to support one another. The same can be said for at home. Gratitude for your spouse, kids, and family leads to more compassion and love, creating a better home environment for all of you as you are focusing on and supporting one another due to your gratitude for each other and the blessings you have.

I know growing and nurturing an attitude of gratitude is difficult for many, but it is a skill and has to be worked on consistently to be developed. Knowing this is challenging for many, up next are some ways to help you work on the skill of gratitude.

How Gratitude Impacts Body, Mind, and Spirit

- Faith: Gratitude reminds us that God is working all things together for good, even when life feels hard. (Romans 8:28)

- Fitness: Shifts mindset from "I have to work out" to "I get to move my body." Instead of focusing on what you can't do yet, gratitude celebrates what you can do.

- Mindset: Gratitude fights stress, anxiety, and self-criticism. It helps you love your body as a gift, wherever you are on the journey.

- Relationships: Gratitude makes you more compassionate, forgiving, and present. It builds unity at home and in community.

The Benefits of Practicing Gratitude

- Boosts Mental Resilience: Helps you see beyond setbacks and recognize growth.

- Strengthens Faith: Keeps you aligned with God's will and focused on His blessings.

- Increases Joy: Shifts your heart from complaining to rejoicing.

- Improves Relationships: Makes you more compassionate, forgiving, and connected to others.

- Enhances Health: Lowers stress, improves sleep, and motivates better self-care.

Reflection Questions

- What are three things you are grateful for right now?

- What is one challenge in your life right now that you can approach with gratitude, and how might that shift your mindset?

- How will daily gratitude help you stay aligned with your purpose?

- Who can you thank today for how they've impacted your life?

- How would living with gratitude change the way you pursue your God-given purpose each day?

Habits to Build Gratitude

Daily Habits:

- Gratitude Journal: Write three things you're thankful for—no repeats! Make it real and personal.

- Start and End with Thanks: Bookend your day with gratitude in prayer.

- Gratitude in Prayer: Before asking God for anything, first thank Him for what He's already done.

Faith and Fitness Habits:

- Before a Workout: Thank God for the ability to move and grow stronger.

- During a Workout: Focus on what your body can do—each rep is a gift.

- After a Workout: Celebrate finishing, even if it was tough.

- Gratitude in Movement: Use walking, stretching, or yoga as moments to reflect on God's blessings.

- Faith-Based Fitness: Pray or meditate during exercise to connect spirit and body. Philippians 4:4-9 reminds us to rejoice always and to pray with thanksgiving, so that God's peace may guard our hearts and minds.

  - Philippians 4:4-9 - "Rejoice in the Lord always; again I will say, rejoice. Let your reasonableness be known to everyone. The Lord is at hand; do not be anxious about anything, but in everything by prayer and supplication with thanksgiving let your requests be made known to God. And the peace of God, which surpasses all understanding, will guard your hearts and your minds in Christ Jesus. Finally, brothers, whatever is true, whatever is honorable, whatever is just, whatever is pure, whatever is lovely, whatever is commendable, if there is any excellence, if there is anything worthy of praise, think about these things. What you have learned and received and heard and seen in me—practice these things, and the God of peace will be with you."

Bringing It Together: Action Steps to Cultivate Gratitude

- Start a Gratitude Journal

    - Each morning or night, write down three things you're thankful for—no repeats. Reflect on small and big blessings, from answered prayers to simple joys like a warm meal or a walk outside.

- Begin Your Day with Thanks

    - Begin your day by thanking God in prayer. End your day by reflecting on where you saw His goodness. This habit will frame your life with faith and gratitude.

- Thank Before You Ask

    - In every prayer, list what you're thankful for before making a single request. Let praise lead the way.

- Move with Gratitude

    - Before your next workout, say, "Thank you, God, for this body." During the workout, focus on what your body can do—not what it can't. Afterward, celebrate showing up, no matter how it went.

- Turn Setbacks into Thankfulness
    - Write down one current challenge and ask: How is God using this for my growth? Gratitude in hard times builds extraordinary resilience.

- Gratitude Walks
    - Take 5–10 minutes to walk in silence and list blessings in your mind—family, nature, purpose, faith. Let your movement be a moment of worship.

- Express It to Others
    - Send a text, write a note, or speak a word of thanks to someone who's impacted your life. Gratitude grows when it's shared.

- Reflect Weekly
    - Each week, review your journal or prayer notes. What are the patterns? Where is God working in your life? Let gratitude fuel a deeper awareness of His faithfulness.

Final Charge: The Impact of Gratitude on Health and Growth

- Motivation and Discipline: Grateful people stick to routines better, because they want to take care of what God has given them.

- Resilience: Helps you bounce back from setbacks—injuries, failures, tough days.

- Recovery and Sleep: Lowers stress and improves rest, critical for body and mind healing.

- Faith and Trust: Deepens reliance on God during hard times. Keeps you hopeful, not discouraged.

- Relationships: Builds compassion, unity, and love—starting at home.

It is easy to get caught up in all the craziness of life and lose sight of all the blessings you have within your life. But to truly lead a fulfilled and purposeful life, the practice of gratitude is a must. Otherwise, you will always be "keeping up with the Joneses," always comparing your lives to others instead of seeing all the amazing blessings that you already have in your life, and working on always finding joy and gratitude with that. This attitude will help bring out the extraordinary you!

Gratitude is not comparing yourself to others; it is reflecting and truly appreciating what your life is blessed with.

Gratitude isn't just a feeling—it's a practice, and that's why it's also a key pillar of The Extraordinary Strength Method™. It turns discipline into joy, struggle into strength, and everyday moments into worship. Gratitude keeps your heart soft, your mind strong, and your body moving forward. It's what reminds you why you're fighting for a better life.

Without gratitude, you'll burn out. With gratitude, you'll rise up. Gratitude isn't just a feeling—it's a choice that unlocks joy, resilience, and extraordinary strength.

This may seem silly or even challenging when just starting to do this, but shifting your mindset to an attitude of gratitude will change so much within your life. By making gratitude a regular practice, you can strengthen both your faith and fitness, creating a balanced approach that nourishes the mind, body, and spirit. By grounding yourself in gratitude, you'll build resilience and strength for the challenges ahead.

Now, here's the thing about gratitude: when you start seeing all the blessings you've received, you won't be able to help but want to give back. Gratitude naturally overflows into generosity. In the next chapter, we'll explore how generosity will multiply your impact and deepen your purpose. Get ready to take what God has given you and use it to bless others to be the extraordinary you.

Pillar 7: Generosity

Generosity—The Heart of Extraordinary Strength

If gratitude is what fills your heart, generosity is what overflows from it.

When you realize how much you've been given, you can't help but give. You can't help but share. Because a life focused only on yourself will always feel empty, but a life poured out for others is where purpose and joy are found.

Generosity is one of the greatest acts of strength you can cultivate. Not strength for yourself—but strength for others.

If you want to know the secret to joy and freedom, start giving. Giving isn't just for those with 'extra'—it's the mark of a strong, purpose-driven life. In a world obsessed with getting, God calls us to give. And when we live generously, something powerful happens: we step into the life of purpose we were designed for.

"But Jesus called them to him and said, 'You know that the rulers of the Gentiles lord it over them, and their great ones exercise authority over them. It shall not be so among you. But whoever would be great among you must be your servant, and whoever would be first among you must be your slave, even as the Son of Man came not to be served but to serve, and to give his life as a ransom for many.'" - Matthew 20:25-28 (ESV)

Generosity Is for You as Much as It Is for Others

Generosity, like gratitude, is a gift to you just as it is a gift to others. In the Bible, generosity is the act of giving away what you have with joy and without hesitation, regardless of wealth. The dictionary defines generous as "showing a readiness to give more of something, as money or time, than is strictly necessary or expected" and "showing kindness toward others." So generosity is a simple act of sharing what you have with joy. This could be tithing, charitable contributions, giving to a friend in need, giving your time, giving your talent, giving your possessions, or giving your wisdom and knowledge. This comes from an overflow of love, not by just how much money you make or have.

Many people think, 'I'll be generous when I have more.' But if you're not generous with a little, you won't be generous with a lot. Generosity is not about the amount; it's about the heart. Mark 12:41-44 (ESV), *"And he sat down opposite the treasury and watched the people putting money into the offering box. Many rich people put in large sums. And a poor widow came and put in two small copper coins, which make a penny. And he called his disciples to him and said to them, 'Truly, I say to you, this poor widow has put in more than all those who are contributing to the offering box. For they all contributed out of their abundance, but she out of her poverty has put in everything she had, all she had to live on.'"*

Jesus is talking about the sacrifice she is making out of love, while the others only gave a small amount of what they truly had. Her overflowing love prompted her to give more of what she had, even if by dollar amounts it was less, she made a much larger sacrifice. When you have generosity like this, you have a different mindset than most of the world, being generous with what you have, not what is left over.

Generosity Starts with Contentment

In the world we live in, acts of kindness and generosity seem to be becoming rarer as people feel the need to elevate themselves on the things that they have over what they are able to give to others. The world struggles with contentment and is always on the search for "more."

> *"But godliness with contentment is great gain, for we brought nothing into the world, and we cannot take anything out of the world." - 1 Timothy 6:6-7 (ESV)*

Being generous has to come from a mindset of transformation, knowing that you are doing something good for somebody else. It should not feel like a duty that has to be done, but motivated by joy in helping others out of love.

Generosity flows from contentment—but fear tries to block it. Fear says, 'What if I don't have enough?' But generosity says, 'God has given me enough to bless someone else.' When we give, we don't lose; we gain freedom, joy, and God's favor. Giving isn't a duty—it's a joyful act of love.

This type of generosity mindset has to come with contentment of what you have and not comparing your life and the things you have to others. Dave Ramsey said, *"No one has ever become poor by giving"* and *"Givers are content because they know that stuff won't make them happy."* He also lists out that:

- Giving is a key part of a healthy budget
- Giving can lead to contentment
- Giving can help heal selfishness
- Giving can make a difference in others' lives

> *"One gives freely, yet grows all the richer; another withholds what he should give, and only suffers want. Whoever brings blessing will be enriched, and one who waters will himself be watered." - Proverbs 11:24-25*

True Generosity Comes from Strength, Not Leftovers

Having a mindset of generosity will help you flourish and experience true joy and happiness as you are blessing others. If this is something new to you, that is okay! Start small. Give of your time, wisdom, or talent. Generosity is a mindset and a skill, so it must be worked on. The more you act on this and give, the easier it becomes and the more joy you will have! True generosity will show the condition of your heart.

Matthew 6:19-21 (ESV) says, *"Do not lay up for yourselves treasures on earth, where moth and rust destroy and where thieves break in and steal, but lay up for yourselves treasures in heaven, where neither moth nor rust destroys and where thieves do not break in and steal. For where your treasure is, there your heart will be also."*

Real generosity doesn't give from what's "left over"—it gives from the first fruits. It's easy to give when you've got extra time or money. But the kind of generosity that changes lives—including your own—costs you something. That's why generosity is a mark of strength—it means you are trusting God enough to give before knowing how it will all work out.

Where you invest—your time, money, energy—reveals your heart. If you want a heart aligned with God's purpose, you've got to start living generously.

Generosity and The Extraordinary Strength Method™

Generosity is a final pillar of The Extraordinary Strength Method™ because true strength isn't just about what you can achieve for yourself, but about how you lift others up. A strong life is an outward-focused life—one that leaves a legacy.

This final mind component of The Extraordinary Strength Method™ is shifting from inward focus to outward purpose—through generosity. Giving is more than an act; it's a powerful mindset that unlocks joy, freedom, and deeper purpose, because true strength is not about what you can get, but what you can give.

You weren't made to live life only for yourself—you were made to overflow into others.

Generosity shifts your focus outward, giving you a bigger reason to be strong, disciplined, and driven—because your life isn't just about your own success. It's about who you're called to serve.

Find joy in contentment and giving to others, and God will continue to bless you abundantly, for you are fulfilling your purpose and becoming that extraordinary you!

Reflection Questions

- Where has fear of "not enough" held you back from being generous?

- How would living generously shift your focus from yourself to your purpose?

- Who can you serve or give to this week—whether with time, talent, or treasure?

- What would change in your life if generosity was a daily habit?

- What does generosity look like in your faith, fitness, and family life?

Habits to Build a Generous Life

Daily Habits

- Give First, Not Last: Whether it's time, energy, or money—set it aside to give before anything else.

- Ask This Question Daily: *"Who can I serve today?"* Look for opportunities to encourage, help, or give.

- Practice Random Acts of Kindness: Leave an encouraging note, pay for someone's coffee, or offer help unexpectedly.

Weekly Habits

- Time Tithing: Commit a percentage of your time each week to serving others—church, family, community.

- Encourage Three People a Week: Text, call, or write to someone to encourage them.

- Generosity Journal: At the end of the week, write one way you gave and how it impacted you.

Bringing It Together: Action Steps to Cultivate Generosity

- Start with What You Have

  - Don't wait for "extra." Choose one way today to give from what you already have—your time, your energy, your resources, or your encouragement. Generosity starts where you are.

- Look for Giving Moments

  - Set aside time each week to give intentionally—whether it's volunteering, writing a note of encouragement, serving at your church, or surprising someone with a kind gesture.

- Give First, Not Last

  - Practice the habit of giving first—whether that's with money (tithing), time (serving), or attention (being fully present). Make giving the first fruit, not the leftover.

- Ask Daily: "Who Can I Serve Today?"

  - This one question can change everything. Ask it each morning and watch how your eyes—and heart—open to opportunities around you.

- Journal the Impact

- At the end of each week, write down one way you gave and how it impacted both the other person and you. Gratitude + generosity builds momentum and joy.

- Start a Legacy List
  - Write a short list of the people or causes you want your life to bless. Let that vision guide how you spend your time, energy, and money each week.

- Practice Silent Giving
  - Do something for someone without telling them. Let your strength be quiet and selfless. This builds humility and deep internal strength.

Final Charge: Generosity Is Strength

Generosity is a spiritual strength that transforms you and the world around you. When you give, you break free from selfishness, scarcity, and fear—and you open yourself to joy, purpose, and the blessings of God.

Giving is a bold declaration that you trust God to provide and that your life is meant to bless others. So if you want to be extraordinary, start living to give.

"It is more blessed to give than to receive." — *Acts 20:35*

When you live with generosity, you gain purpose. You begin to live beyond yourself, making an impact in the lives of others. But to fully step into that extraordinary version of yourself, you need to bring together everything we've talked about—belief, discipline, gratitude, responsibility, generosity, and the ability to endure when life gets hard.

So before we move on to strengthening the body, let's pull it all together. In the next chapter, we'll revisit how these mindsets work together to build unshakable strength—mentally, spiritually, and emotionally—so you are fully equipped for the road ahead.

Because becoming extraordinary starts in the mind—but it doesn't stop there. Get ready to put it all together and prepare for the next phase of your journey.

The Call to Extraordinary — Building the Mindset for Purpose and Perseverance

God has a purpose for your life, and He created you to be extraordinary. But becoming that extraordinary version of yourself requires more than just desire or fleeting motivation—it requires intentional effort, discipline, belief, and the ability to lean into discomfort. It requires a mindset grounded in responsibility, values, gratitude, generosity, and unwavering perseverance.

This transformation doesn't happen overnight. It's a journey that encompasses your mind, body, and spirit, requiring you to align your actions with your purpose and grow stronger from the inside out. By cultivating belief, discipline, responsibility, gratitude, generosity, and a tolerance for discomfort, you can become the person God designed you to be.

Recapping the Path to an Extraordinary Mind

So far, we've laid the foundation of what it takes to master your mind and step into your God-given calling:

Belief is where it all begins. You must believe that transformation is possible and that God has already equipped you for the life you are meant to live. Without belief, nothing else will stand. Through daily affirmations, scripture, and surrounding yourself with people of faith, you strengthen this core pillar.

You've confronted the fear of failure, learning that fear is not a stop sign—it's an invitation to grow. You've reframed fear as a teacher, and now, you move forward even when the outcome is uncertain.

You've embraced responsibility, recognizing that while not everything is your fault, everything is your responsibility to handle and move forward. Taking ownership of your life, choices, and habits is where true transformation begins.

You've examined and defined your values and standards, realizing that what you stand for shapes how you live. When you live by high standards and refuse to settle, you create a life of purpose and meaning.

You've leaned into discipline and discomfort, recognizing that motivation will fail, but discipline and resilience carry you through. You've chosen to do the hard things now so that life gets better later—and you've realized that discomfort is the training ground of growth.

You've cultivated an attitude of gratitude, understanding that gratitude fuels perseverance. Gratitude transforms the way you face challenges, giving you joy and endurance when life feels heavy.

And finally, you've embraced generosity, shifting from an inward focus to an outward purpose. Giving your time, talent, and treasure is part of what makes you extraordinary, because a life lived only for oneself is small—but a life lived for others is expansive and filled with purpose.

Through it all, perseverance and endurance have been quietly working beneath the surface. You've learned that true strength is staying the course when things get hard. It's getting back up when you fall, and pressing on when you feel like giving up.

> *"Let us not grow weary of doing good, for in due season we will reap, if we do not give up."* - Galatians 6:9 (ESV)

Throughout this section, we've uncovered seven pillars of The Extraordinary Strength Method™ that form the foundation for becoming the person God created you to be. Now, as we close this section, it's time to bring these pillars together and see how they align with purpose and perseverance—so you are equipped to keep going when life gets hard.

The Eight Pillars of Mental Strength for an Extraordinary Life

Becoming the extraordinary version of yourself—strong in mind, body, and spirit—starts right here: in the mind. But not just with surface-level thinking. You need mental strength rooted in biblical truth and daily action.

These eight pillars make up the mental framework of The Extraordinary Strength Method™. If you want to walk in your purpose, you have to build your mind around these principles—because when your mind is right, your life will follow.

Pillar 1: Belief—The Fuel for Transformation

Before anything can change around you, something has to shift within you. Belief is where that shift begins. You must believe not only that you are capable of becoming extraordinary, but that God has already equipped you to do so.

Belief isn't just wishful thinking—it's the foundation that every action is built on.

"As a man thinks in his heart, so is he."
— Proverbs 23:7 (NKJV)

Action Reflection:

- What limiting beliefs are currently shaping your actions?
- What does God say is true about you?
- Are you walking like someone who believes you are called and equipped?

Pillar 2: Fear of Failure—Learning to Fail Forward

Most people stop before they start because of fear—especially the fear of failure. But failure isn't final. It's the process of success. Every stumble is a setup for growth, if you're willing to learn from it.

Your failures are not disqualifications—they are training grounds for your calling.

"For though the righteous fall seven times, they rise again." — Proverbs 24:16 (NIV)

Action Reflection:

- What are you afraid to fail at—and why?

- What have you learned from your past failures?

- What would change if you saw failure as feedback instead of final?

Pillar 3: Responsibility—Own Your Life

Nothing in this book works without ownership. You can't outsource your growth. Your mindset, your actions, your health, your faith—it's all on you.

Some things may not be your fault, but they are your responsibility.

> *"For each will have to bear his own load."* — Galatians 6:5 (ESV)

Action Reflection:

- Where are you blaming others or your circumstances?

- What part of your life do you need to take full responsibility for?

- What changes when you stop waiting for someone else to fix it?

Pillar 4: Values and Standards— Define What You Stand For

If you don't clearly define what matters most to you, the world will decide for you. And let's be real—the world's standards are painfully low.

You were made to live by God's values, not culture's comfort. Your values drive your decisions, your habits, and your legacy.

> *"Do not be conformed to this world, but be transformed by the renewal of your mind..."* — *Romans 12:2 (ESV)*

Action Reflection:

- What are your non-negotiable values?
- Are your current habits and choices aligned with them?
- Where have you allowed your standards to be lowered?

Pillar 5: Discipline & Discomfort– Choose the Harder Right

Discipline is doing what needs to be done, even when you don't feel like it. And you build it by embracing discomfort—not running from it. That's where the real growth is.

Extraordinary strength isn't built in the comfort zone.

> *"But I discipline my body and keep it under control..."* — *1 Corinthians 9:27 (ESV)*

Action Reflection:

- Where are you avoiding discomfort?

- What small disciplines can you commit to daily?

- How would your life look different if you got comfortable being uncomfortable?

Pillar 6: Gratitude—Fuel for the Journey

Gratitude isn't just a feeling—it's a choice that reframes your entire perspective. It turns your workouts into worship. Your obstacles into opportunities. Your struggles into strength.

When you stop focusing on what you lack and start thanking God for what you have, everything changes.

> *"Give thanks in all circumstances; for this is the will of God in Christ Jesus for you."* — *1 Thessalonians 5:18 (ESV)*

Action Reflection:

- What are three things you're thankful for today?

- How does gratitude shift the way you view your current struggle?

- How would your energy and effort change if you approached every day with thanksgiving?

Pillar 7: Generosity—The Overflow of Strength

True strength isn't about how much you can lift—it's about how much you can give. When you realize how blessed you are, generosity becomes your response.

You don't wait to have more to give. You give because God has already given you enough.

> *"It is more blessed to give than to*
> *receive." — Acts 20:35 (ESV)*

Action Reflection:

- Where can you be more generous—with your time, energy, or resources?

- Who can you serve today with no expectation in return?

- What would shift if your default mindset was generosity?

Now let's finish with the final pillar that has been a common thread through all of the previous pillars: perseverance.

Pillar 8: Perseverance

Perseverance: The Thread that Binds It All Together

These pillars are powerful, but without perseverance, they crumble under pressure. Perseverance is the glue that holds it all together.

Perseverance is defined as *"persistence in doing something despite difficulty or delay in achieving success."*

In the Bible, perseverance refers to the steadfast endurance and continued effort to live a life pleasing to God, especially when facing challenges or trials. It involves not giving up on one's faith and spiritual goals, even when circumstances are difficult or discouraging

Life is going to test you. You will face seasons when belief falters, discipline wanes, and gratitude feels impossible. That's why perseverance is the final, essential mindset. It's the decision to keep going no matter what.

> *"Consider it pure joy, my brothers and sisters, whenever you face trials of many kinds, because you know that the testing of your faith produces perseverance. Let perseverance finish its work so that you may be mature and complete, not lacking anything." — James 1:2-4 (NIV)*

When you live by responsibility, values, belief, gratitude, generosity, and discipline, perseverance becomes possible. And when you persevere, you become mature, complete, and equipped to fulfill your God-given purpose.

Reflection Questions:

- Where in your life have you given up too soon?
- What would it look like to persevere through the current challenge you're facing?
- How can you prepare your mind now to endure future trials?

Habits to Build Perseverance

- Start with a Daily "Don't Quit" Reminder
  - Each morning, declare: "I will keep going, even when it's hard." Post this where you'll see it—your mirror, desk, or lock screen.

- Push Through One More Rep
  - Whether it's in your workout, your work, or your spiritual walk—do one more than you feel like. One more rep. One more page. One more act of faith.

- Embrace the Hard Days
  - When it gets tough, pause and say: "This is where I become extraordinary." Train your mind to see resistance as growth—not failure.

- Track the Streak, Not Just the Wins
  - Create a perseverance tracker. Mark each day you showed up—regardless of results. The habit of showing up is the victory.

- Reflect on Past Battles You've Already Won
  - Remind yourself of the times you didn't give up. Write them down. You've overcome before—you can do it again.

- Create a Perseverance Anchor Verse
  - Choose a Scripture like James 1:2–4 or Romans 5:3–5 and write it somewhere visible. Recite it when you feel like quitting.

- Set Mini Milestones
  - Break big goals into small, winnable steps. Celebrate each one. This builds momentum and mental toughness.

- Identify a Current Challenge You're Tempted to Quit

  - Write it down. Then list one small action step you'll take today to keep going.

- Prepare for the Storm Before It Hits

  - Build your mental strength daily—through prayer, Scripture, movement, and truth—so when trials come, your foundation stands firm.

- Anchor in God's Promises

  - When you're tested, cling to Scripture—not your feelings. Let God's truth carry you forward when motivation fades.

- Choose Purpose Over Comfort

  - Every time you choose purpose instead of ease, you strengthen your perseverance muscle. Ask, "What does my purpose require of me today?"

- Reframe Failure as Fuel

  - When you fall short, don't stop. Step back, learn, and recommit. Progress is built through pressure.

- Lean Into Support

  - Perseverance doesn't mean doing it alone. Reach out, ask for help, and surround yourself with those who want to see you win.

- Make Perseverance a Non-Negotiable
  - Decide now: "I finish what I start." Let your actions prove it, even when emotions don't want to cooperate.

Final Charge: Don't Quit—You're Closer Than You Think

You've built belief, embraced discipline, taken responsibility, rooted yourself in values, practiced gratitude, lived generously—and now comes the test: Will you keep going when it's hard?

This is where most people stop. But not you.

You've come too far to only come this far.

Perseverance is what transforms good intentions into a strong legacy. It's what refines your character, proves your faith, and sharpens your calling. And it's what separates the average from the extraordinary.

So, when you're tired, remember your purpose. When you're discouraged, remember who walks beside you. When you feel like giving up, go one more step.

God doesn't waste pain—He uses it to produce perseverance, and that perseverance will finish its work in you.

You are stronger than you think. You are not alone. And you are being prepared for something greater.

So don't quit now. Your purpose and the extraordinary you is waiting.

The Final Call: Rise into the Extraordinary You

The journey to the extraordinary you starts with the mind but cannot stay there. A renewed mind lays the foundation, but it is only the beginning. Without action, belief fades. Without discipline, intentions die. That's why mastering your mind must be followed by strengthening your body.

A strong mind must be matched by a strong body. The mind fuels discipline, but the body carries it out. You can renew your mindset, but without physical strength and energy, taking action becomes impossible.

But before we move forward, there's something critical you need to understand: If even one of the cornerstones are missing, your life will feel misaligned. Your foundation will be cracked, and that crack will eventually limit your growth. Let's reflect on this truth from the introduction:

- Strong Mind but weak Body = Vision without execution

- Strong Body but weak Mind = Action without direction

- Strong Mind and Body but weak Spirit = Burnout and emptiness

- All three without Purpose = Strength without impact

These aren't just clever phrases—they're real consequences that prevent people from ever stepping into their God-given potential.

1. Strong Mind but Weak Body = Vision Without Execution

You've now developed the mindset: belief, discipline, responsibility, gratitude, generosity, perseverance. But if your body lacks the strength and energy to act on those convictions, you'll find yourself frustrated and stuck.

You'll know what to do—but be too exhausted, unhealthy, or physically unprepared to do it.

You'll dream big—but your body will hold you back.

You'll want to lead—but your health will limit your ability to serve.

Your mindset fuels your purpose, but your body is the vessel that carries it out. Without a strong body, your extraordinary vision remains just a vision—never fully lived out.

2. Strong Body but Weak Mind = Action Without Direction

On the flip side, many people train their bodies but never master their minds. They have strength—but lack purpose. They're disciplined in the gym—but undisciplined in thought. They push themselves physically—but crumble under pressure or discouragement. Without mental strength, their actions become scattered, reactive, and hollow.

That's why Cornerstone 1 comes first.

Without a renewed, focused, faith-filled mind, the body is just movement without mission.

You don't just need action—you need aligned action.

But when the mind and body come together—when mindset is fueled by belief and executed with strength—your life begins to move forward with power and clarity.

This is why the Extraordinary Strength Method™ builds on all four cornerstones. Because your life wasn't meant to be partially powerful—it was meant to be wholly aligned, mind, body, spirit, and purpose.

So as we move into the next cornerstone, we're going to shift from mastering your mind to mastering your body. You'll learn how to build a vessel that is strong, resilient, and prepared to carry out the mission God has given you.

These eight pillars aren't just concepts—they're skills. And like any skill, they get stronger the more you practice them.

> *"Not only that, but we rejoice in our sufferings,*
> *knowing that suffering produces endurance, and*
> *endurance produces character, and character*
> *produces hope."* — *Romans 5:3-4 (ESV)*

So here's your call to action:

Don't just read these—live them. Build them into your life. Train them daily.

Because mastering your mind is the first step to unlocking your God-given potential. But it's not the last.

Now that your mind is being renewed, strengthened, and aligned with purpose, it's time to take the next step.

Your body is the vessel that carries out the mission.

Your body is where faith becomes action.

And your physical strength is about to be built on the foundation we've just laid.

Get ready to build the body that can carry out your calling. The mind has been strengthened; now it's time to forge the body—next up is Cornerstone Two: Strengthen Your Body.

Let's go.

Strengthen Your Body (Physical Strength)

Now that you have hopefully reflected on where you stand with your mind through your values, self beliefs, and structures of your mind, it is time to put some of that to work and take action. Your body is the house of your mind, and if it is not healthy, then the mind will start to fail as well. Your body is the one thing you get to take with you all of your life, and yet it is the one thing most will neglect and not take care of.

So many people believe that owning materials in life are "needed." The newest phone, the nicest car, a bigger TV, and so on. In the end, your body is the only true thing you own, so why not take care of it like you would the things in life that you buy? When your body fails, your life is over and all those material things will either get sold or go in the trash. Your body is the most valuable thing you own in your life, so your health has to be a priority.

Working out has always been a part of my life in some way. I grew up playing outside, working outside, doing manual labor, and was always involved in some sport any chance I could get. I loved physical activity. It was something I felt I was great at.

Then I was told by my high school football coach that I was not big enough to play college football, so I didn't even try. Going into college, I still worked out with my friends and played a bunch of sports, but then that season of my life hit when everything went sideways. I was blessed to have some friends that got me back into the gym, and in that time of my life, that became my religion, until I dedicated my life to Christ. But at that point, the gym was my church.

Training my body helped me train my mind. It went hand in hand. When I wasn't taking care of my body, I was stuck in depression, my grades were trash, and everything in my head just seemed like it was in a fog. All of that changed as I started training again.

I was able to get off of the antidepressants, started enjoying my schooling again, increased my grades, and my confidence rose with it as well. The more I trained my body, the better my mind got. Everything in life became clearer, including my purpose. But as stated before, I found I was missing something, and that was my relationship with God. Training my body and taking care of my health led me to my salvation and my purpose.

Paul says it so well in 1 Corinthians 6:19-20 (ESV), "*Or do you not know that your body is a temple of the Holy Spirit within you, whom you have from God? You are not your own, for you were bought with a price. So glorify God in your body.*"

You only get one body, one life, why would you treat your body horribly and not take care of it? When your body fails, you lose your life. Some lose it way earlier than they should because they never take care of their body. They never get to fulfill their purpose.

As children of God, we are called to take care of our temple so we may serve and glorify God. The good news is that there is never a time that you cannot change things and begin taking care of your body. It doesn't matter where you are at in your life, the perfect time is right now. You cannot change the past, but you can change what you are doing today to change your future.

Your body is the vessel God gave you to live out your purpose—and yet, for many, it's the most neglected part of their life. You get one body for life, and when it fails, your mission stops. If you want to become the extraordinary you, it's time to treat your body like the gift and tool that it is.

You can't fully strengthen your mind and spirit if your body is falling apart. You need a body that can carry out God's mission for you—one that has energy, endurance, and strength.

In this section, we'll break down three key pillars to strengthen your body:

- Training
- Nutrition
- Body Composition

Each one is critical to building the physical strength and energy required to fulfill your God-given purpose.

Pillar 1: Training

Building Strength for Life and Purpose

*"Therefore, I urge you, brothers and sisters, in
view of God's mercy, to offer your bodies as a living
sacrifice, holy and pleasing to God—this is your true
and proper worship."* – Romans 12:1 (NIV)

Training is one of the foundational pillars of The Extraordinary Strength Method™—our system for building the strength to live fully in body, mind, and spirit. We train not just for looks or performance, but for life—to have the strength, endurance, and resilience to serve God, our families, and our communities well.

Training is for everyone, regardless of age, gender, or fitness level. We train not just for looks or performance, but for life—to have the strength, endurance, and resilience to serve God, our families, and our communities.

Your body is a tool God has given you to fulfill your mission. You can't fully live out His purpose if you're too weak or sick to show up.

Training is for Every Age and Every Stage

There is no age that cannot train to better their body and health. We have repeatedly proven this in our gym. Our youngest client was three years old when she began and our oldest was ninety-four. As I write this, I am currently training my grandparents who are eighty-seven and eighty-five, and they are absolutely amazing! They live on their own and can literally do anything they want to. Here is the thing, though, they only started training with me three years ago. Up to that point, they have stayed active and taken care of their body throughout their lives. My grandpa even worked full-time until he was eighty-three, just because he could and he loved what he did. It has nothing to do with their genes and everything to do with their daily actions.

So let me say this clearly: age is no excuse.

Why Training Matters for Everyone

Many people think training is only for athletes or those chasing a fitness goal. But most people are training for life—to have the strength to handle daily tasks, take care of their families, and live with energy and confidence.

Unfortunately, most people live sedentary lives, and without intentional physical stress (through exercise), the body breaks down faster than it should.

"If you don't make time for wellness, you'll be forced to make time for illness."

As we age, our body atrophies faster and faster, meaning muscles, bone density, heart health, and lung capacity start to diminish and worsen without proper training and stress put on it to help it get stronger. So without physical labor in our daily lives, it has to be something we intentionally do to have the best quality of life.

There are times in our lives that we may not have the capability to train four to six hours per week, but intentional activity is still something we can get without being in a gym working out. Every person should strive for 10,000 steps per day, whether they are going to the gym to train or not. Our society is so sedentary that the average person gets only 3,000 to 4,000 steps per day. But you don't want to be average, you want to be extraordinary! We train so our bodies are strong enough to serve God and fulfill our purpose.

Training is Worship

As Paul says in Romans 12:1, our bodies are a living sacrifice—and training is one way we worship God with our bodies. How you treat your body reflects how you honor Him. When you take care of your body, you're honoring God and preparing yourself to serve others.

> *"After all, no one ever hated their own body, but they feed and care for their body, just as Christ does the church." — Ephesians 5:29 (NIV)*

Your body, mind, and spirit are deeply connected. Neglecting one affects the others. That's why training is about more than muscles—it's about honoring the gift God has given you and preparing yourself for the mission He has for you.

Training your body has immense benefits for the mind, body, and spirit! Let's hit some simple, yet impactful benefits of training!

The Benefits of Training – Body, Mind, and Spirit

For Your Body

1) Improved physical health. Regular exercise strengthens the cardiovascular system, builds muscle, improves flexibility, and enhances endurance. It reduces the risk of chronic diseases such as heart disease, diabetes, and obesity. We will hit on this more throughout this section.

2) Increased Energy Levels: Physical activity boosts energy by improving circulation and increasing oxygen flow to tissues, making daily activities easier and more efficient.

3) Weight and Body Composition Management: Exercise helps in maintaining a healthy weight by burning calories and building muscle, which in turn boosts metabolism.

4) Enhanced Immune Function: Regular physical activity strengthens the immune system, helping the body fight off illnesses more effectively.

5) Better Sleep Quality: Exercise helps regulate sleep patterns, leading to deeper and more restful sleep, which is crucial for overall health.

For Your Mind

1) Reduced Stress and Anxiety: Physical activity reduces levels of the body's stress hormones, such as adrenaline and cortisol, while stimulating the production of endorphins, which act as natural mood lifters.

2) Improved Cognitive Function: Regular exercise has been shown to improve memory, attention, and processing speed. It promotes the growth of new brain cells and enhances overall brain function.

3) Enhanced Mood: Exercise releases neurotransmitters like serotonin and dopamine, which are associated with happiness and a sense of well-being, reducing the risk of depression.

4) Increased Mental Resilience: Regular physical activity helps develop mental toughness and resilience, enabling better coping with life's challenges.

5) Boosted Confidence and Self-Esteem: Achieving fitness goals, improving physical appearance, and gaining strength can lead to higher self-esteem and a more positive self-image.

For Your Spirit

1) Mind-Body Connection: Exercise like weight lifting, metabolic training, and mindful walking, can deepen the connection between the mind and body, promoting spiritual awareness and presence.

2) Spiritual Discipline and Growth: Consistent physical activity requires discipline, which can translate into spiritual discipline, fostering growth in areas like patience, perseverance, and self-control.

3) Stress Relief and Inner Peace: Physical activity can serve as a form of meditation or mindfulness, providing a space for reflection, prayer, and helping to quiet the mind, leading to better time with God and better internal peace.

4) Sense of Purpose and Fulfillment: Regular exercise routines can contribute to a sense of purpose and accomplishment, aligning with spiritual goals of self-improvement and fulfilling God's purpose for your life.

5) Community and Connection: Engaging in group activities like team sports, fitness classes, or community events can

foster a sense of belonging and connection, which is a key aspect of spiritual life.

Training your body helps align your mind and spirit—so you can show up fully for the mission God has for you.

Training for Life: Mind, Body, and Spirit

Reflection Questions:

- How can you intentionally incorporate physical activity (like daily steps) as an act of worship?

- How has training impacted your mental and spiritual well-being?

- What steps can you take to align your fitness journey with your faith and purpose?

- How can you create community and connection through shared fitness experiences?

Habits to Build

- Daily Activity: Aim for 10,000 steps per day to stay active— even on rest days.

- Strength Training: Incorporate 2-3 strength sessions per week to maintain muscle and bone health.

- Mind-Body Connection: Use training and walking as intentional, mindful movement—a time for prayer and reflection.

- Consistency Over Perfection: Stay committed to regular movement—this is a lifelong practice, not a seasonal hobby.

- Spiritual Alignment: See your body as a sacred gift from God, and honor it through movement.
- Community Engagement: Join group classes or train with others to build relationships and stay accountable.

Bringing It Together: Training in Action

- Take Inventory: What is one area where your physical health is holding you back from living out your purpose?
- Pick Your Movement Plan: Choose 2–3 types of movement you enjoy—strength, walking, hiking, classes—and commit to doing them weekly.
- Set a Step Goal: Track your steps for one week and aim to increase gradually toward 10,000 daily.
- Pray Through Movement: Choose one workout this week to dedicate as a time of prayer, worship, or gratitude.
- Find a Fitness Partner: Invite someone to join you on your training journey for encouragement and accountability.
- Schedule It: Block time in your calendar each week for movement—treat it like a meeting with God and yourself.

Final Charge: Train for Purpose

Training isn't just about looking good—it's about being strong enough to carry out your calling. Your body is the vessel that carries the mission forward. When you train with intention, you're not just building strength—you're building faith, discipline, and purpose.

By embracing these training habits, you'll build strength for life and purpose—gaining not only a healthier body but a stronger mind and spirit to serve God and others.

This is why Training is a pillar of The Extraordinary Strength Method™—because extraordinary purpose requires extraordinary strength.

So don't wait until you feel ready.

Don't wait for the perfect time.

Start now.

Train your body to serve your purpose—because a strong mind needs a strong body to back it up.

Now that we've laid the foundation for why training matters, let's dive deeper into Cardiovascular Endurance, and how building endurance in the gym parallels building perseverance in life and faith.

Cardiovascular Endurance (The Extraordinary Strength Method™ Way)

> *"Not only that, but we rejoice in our sufferings, knowing that suffering produces endurance, and endurance produces character, and character produces hope." – Romans 5:3-4 (ESV)*

In The Extraordinary Strength Method™, cardiovascular endurance is the "engine" that keeps you moving forward—physically, mentally, and spiritually.

Endurance is about more than just getting through a workout. It's about becoming the person God created you to be—someone who keeps going when life gets tough. You can't fulfill your purpose, serve others, or lead well if you lack the stamina to endure. Endurance, both physically and spiritually, is essential to becoming the extraordinary you.

Endurance Is Built Through Challenge

Endurance is as much a mental challenge as it is a physical challenge. Your mentality will either tell you to give up or keep going. Our mind usually gives up way before our body does. That's why building endurance is one of the core pillars of The Extraordinary Strength Method™—because discipline, grit, and perseverance are forged through challenge and discomfort. Just as Paul says in Romans 5, endurance is produced through suffering and that produces character. We train endurance because life demands it—and purpose requires it.

One of the great ways to help your mental fortitude and endurance is by physically working it and challenging it. Training your body to have better cardiovascular endurance takes a lot of grit, and it will help you overcome your own self-limiting belief in what you are capable of. This area of the body is very important not just for your physical health, but for all areas of your life. When you train your body to endure, you're also training your mind to push past self-limiting beliefs and excuses. That kind of mental toughness carries over into your faith, teaching you how to stay strong when life gets hard.

What Is Cardiovascular Endurance?

Cardiovascular endurance is the ability of the heart, lungs, and blood vessels to deliver oxygen to your body tissues during prolonged physical activity. Simply put, it's your body's capacity to keep going—whether during a workout, a long day of service, or a season of trials.

If you're just starting, it's okay to begin small—everyone starts somewhere. You don't have to run a marathon or even a mile to start building endurance. And while running is great, it's not the only way—or even the best way for most people.

Why Interval Training Works Best

With The Extraordinary Strength Method™, we prefer interval-style training because it's adaptable, efficient, and effective for all fitness levels.

How Interval Training Works (The Extraordinary Strength Way):

Intervals = short bursts of effort followed by rest

For example:

- 4–6 movements in a circuit
- Thirty seconds of work, thirty seconds of rest
- Adjust work/rest ratios based on your level (e.g., 20/40 for beginners, 40/20 for advanced)

Interval training is more than efficient; it trains the heart and lungs to work harder and recover faster—like putting your engine through speed drills to increase performance.

Bonus: It burns more calories in less time than traditional steady-state cardio and can be modified to your level. But it should be challenging. You don't want to fully recover between movements—you want to push your limits safely and effectively.

Though running is a great way to burn calories, it typically takes a longer time of activity and could be more stressful on the body due to the amount of impact of running. This does not mean running is bad, but you have to make the proper and safe choice for yourself, based on where you are in your fitness level.

Interval training works so well because we rapidly increase the heart rate and then bring it back down over and over again. A comparison I like to use is that of driving a car down the interstate. If you floor it in your car to get to 100 mph, then slow down to 45 mph, and then back up and down over and over again, how is your fuel efficiency? Terrible! You are expending way more fuel.

Well, your body works the same way. It needs to send more fuel (calories) to the muscles and body to perform at that intensity while the heart rate increases, and then more fuel to help the body recover from that intensity. Whereas running is more like cruise control. It is more fuel-efficient, and you can maintain a certain pace for a longer period of time. So, though running is a great and healthy activity, it may not be the best choice for someone who has less time or needs to worry about impact on their body.

Why Endurance Training Matters
(for the Extraordinary You)

So what are the major benefits of cardiovascular training? Well, improved heart health, increased stamina, reduced risk of heart disease, fat loss, and better overall endurance are some simple ones to start with.

The American Heart Association states that one person dies every thirty-three seconds from heart disease. People in their forties, thirties, and even twenties are having heart attacks. The crazy thing is that most heart disease, especially at younger ages, is preventable by proper training and nutrition.

Along with the other benefits, wouldn't you like to prevent yourself from dying early due to a preventable disease? I would pray the answer is yes. So the answer is right there for you, if you want better heart and lung health, you need to have cardiovascular exercise throughout your week.

The recommendation is 1–3 days per week. If you are new to it, start slow, then as it becomes a habit, start making a couple of those days more intentionally intense.

Metabolic training also helps train your mental toughness and grit. High intensity training and endurance training can be mentally challenging, especially when doing longer bouts of training. Your brain will likely tell you to slow down, lower your intensity, or even stop, because you are feeling tired and because it is hard. This is a great way to build your fortitude to better fight those challenges outside of training. You are way more capable than you think and pushing yourself a little more each day and each time you train will show you that. It should not be comfortable, it should be challenging. If it doesn't challenge you, it doesn't change you.

Don't let yourself stop short. Becoming the extraordinary you means that you have to continue digging deeper and pushing those self-limiting boundaries to become better every day!

Spiritual Endurance – Training for Life's Hardest Battles

Just as we train for physical endurance, we must train for spiritual endurance. You can't expect to thrive spiritually if you never practice. As cardiovascular endurance is developed through proper training, spiritual endurance is developed through regular practices like prayer, meditation, and reading God's word.

Just as cardiovascular endurance builds physical stamina, consistent spiritual practices build resilience and perseverance in faith. If you are not where you want to be with your spiritual endurance, it has to be trained just like anything else. There are many things in life that will test your spiritual endurance, so training for that perseverance is crucial to not give in.

> *"Consider it pure joy, my brothers and sisters, whenever*
> *you face trials of many kinds, because you know that*
> *the testing of your faith produces perseverance. Let*
> *perseverance finish its work so that you may be mature and*
> *complete, not lacking anything." – James 1:2-4 (NIV)*

Spiritual endurance is built through prayer, Scripture, and obedience—especially in hard times. And just like physical training, it takes repetition and consistency to grow stronger.

My Story – Endurance Through Life's Hardest Seasons

Many lose their faith through hardships and challenges of this world, I know I did in the past. I was not prepared for the challenge, and my faith was weak at that point. But, that failure taught me a lot in life and has now helped me to be more resilient and strong in my faith and trust in God.

A little over a year after I had rededicated my life to Christ, my mom was diagnosed with cancer. The emotions from that were intense, but the one thing I did not do was get mad at God or blame God.

Learning from my past, training my body and mind, and developing a stronger relationship with Christ through going to church, praying, and reading His word helped me to have spiritual endurance through that time. There was a peace to it that I could not explain and when I was not sure what to do, I prayed and asked God to help.

I struggled with wanting to do things myself and just handle things on my own, but each time I tried I would get humbled and realize that without Him, I could not do anything. My faith grew stronger through my moms battle with cancer.

There were many ups and downs through the nine years she battled, and many times that we thought she wasn't going to make it, but those harder times helped build my perseverance in my faith and to trust Christ with everything.

As I am writing this, it has been over a year since my mom passed away. That was the hardest part of my life so far. Earlier in my life, this would have sent me over the edge. I would have more than likely taken my own life, but God's plan is so beautiful for us. He had helped prepare me for that time, helped me build my spiritual endurance so I was able to have peace with all that was going on, and to then help my family navigate this time.

Other than my grandmother, I am the only one in my family with any faith, so God had prepared me to help them through this time and gave me the strength and ability to do so. If it was not for all the previous challenges in my life, I would not have had the spiritual endurance and perseverance to do so. Through prayer, Scripture, and reliance on God, I found strength to walk with my family through that storm.

Endurance isn't built in a day—but it's built before you need it. That's why you train, and that's why you prepare. It is something that has to be built on, day after day, challenge after challenge. So start small. Start with just prayer time. It doesn't need to be ten minutes long, but just giving thanksgiving to God and having conversation with Him.

You will have to be intentional about it at first before it becomes a habit and then a behavior, but the more you keep at it, the more natural it becomes, and you will feel that relationship with Him building stronger. Just like with anything with your health, it will not happen overnight, but will continue to grow and increase the more you do. Little upon a little builds a lot over time! Building cardiovascular and spiritual endurance will help you become the extraordinary you and fulfill your purpose!

Cardiovascular Training as a Spiritual Discipline

Cardiovascular endurance strengthens the heart, lungs, and blood vessels, essential for overall physical health and stamina. Just as physical endurance is built through consistent training, spiritual endurance develops through regular practices like prayer, faith, and obedience. Both require pushing past mental barriers and self-limiting beliefs, as endurance is not just a physical challenge but a mental one too. The key to building endurance is starting small and gradually increasing intensity over time, physically and spiritually.

When you push through a tough workout, you're not just training muscles—you're training your mind and spirit to persevere. And when you commit to prayer, reading God's Word, and living with discipline, you're training the spiritual endurance needed to face life's hardest moments.

> *"But those who hope in the Lord will renew their strength. They will soar on wings like eagles; they will run and not grow weary, they will walk and not be faint." – Isaiah 40:31 (NIV)*

Key Benefits of Cardiovascular Endurance Training (The Extraordinary Strength Method™ Style):

Physical:

- Improved heart and lung capacity
- Increased stamina and energy for life's demands
- Reduced risk of heart disease and chronic illness
- Increased fat loss and healthier body composition

Mental:

- Mental toughness and resilience
- Overcoming self-limiting beliefs

- Sharper focus and clarity

Spiritual:

- Perseverance in faith through trials
- Deeper trust and reliance on God
- Spiritual growth through consistent discipline

Reflection Questions

- What mental barriers prevent you from pushing physically or spiritually?
- How can you practice perseverance in your workouts—and your faith?
- What small step will you take this week to build endurance physically and spiritually?
- How has discomfort led to growth in your faith or health journey?
- In what ways do you need to prepare now—physically and spiritually—for the challenges ahead?

Habits to Build: Physical and Spiritual Endurance

Physical Habits:

- 1–3 Days of Interval Training
  - Choose efficient, low-impact formats if needed. Use 30s work/30s rest and adjust intensity weekly.
- Walk Daily

- Aim for 10,000 steps even on rest days—start with what's manageable.

- Progress Gradually

  - Add time, intensity, or complexity every 1–2 weeks.

- Push Your Threshold

  - When your mind says stop, do 1 more rep, 1 more minute. Get uncomfortable.

- Consistency is Key:

  - Stick to a regular schedule—physically and spiritually.

Spiritual Habits:

- Daily Prayer Habit

  - Begin with 2–5 minutes. Make it a time of thanksgiving, surrender, and connection with God.

- Scripture Endurance Plan

  - Focus on passages about perseverance (e.g., James 1:2–4, Romans 5:3–4, Isaiah 40:31).

- Reflect During Physical Training

  - Use your cardio time for prayer, reflection, or worship.

- Spiritual Fasting or Sacrifice
  - Regularly remove distractions to strengthen reliance on God.

Bringing It Together: Endurance in Action

- Pick 1 New Physical Challenge
  - Choose one workout this week that will intentionally test your endurance. Show up and finish it—even when it's hard.

- Anchor to a Verse
  - Before a workout, read and meditate on a Scripture (e.g., Isaiah 40:31). Let it be your fuel.

- Create a Weekly Endurance Plan
  - Schedule 1–3 days of cardio. Be specific about time, type, and intensity. Then stick to it.

- Train Your Spirit Alongside Your Body
  - Pair your hardest workout of the week with a devotional or prayer time afterward.

- Document the Wins
  - Journal one moment each week where you pushed past comfort—physically or spiritually—and how it grew your endurance.

Final Charge: Endurance is at the Heart of Becoming Extraordinary

Endurance is what keeps you in the fight when others give up. It's what turns pain into perseverance, challenge into character, and exhaustion into hope.

In The Extraordinary Strength Method™, training for endurance is training for life—because life will challenge you, and you need the strength to finish your race. Your endurance is your edge. It's what will carry you through life's trials, fulfill your God-given purpose, and help others do the same.

> *"Let us run with endurance the race that is set before us, looking to Jesus, the founder and perfecter of our faith..."* — Hebrews 12:1-2 (ESV)

If you want to be ready for life's storms, you have to start training now—in both body and spirit.

You won't always feel like it, but as you keep going, you'll discover strength you didn't know you had.

When you build endurance, you're not just building fitness—you're building faith, grit, and the extraordinary strength to fulfill your calling.

Muscular Strength (The Extraordinary Strength Method™ Way)

"And you shall love the Lord your God with all your heart and with all your soul and with all your strength." – Mark 12:30

Strength is Worship. Strength is Purpose. Strength is for Everyone.

In The Extraordinary Strength Method™, strength is more than muscles—it's a way to worship God and live out your purpose.

We are called to be strong for the Lord and with God, and that means training both our bodies and our spirits to be strong, resilient, and prepared for the purpose He has given us. Strength is part of how we honor God, serve others, and live fully. It is a way we show our love to God and is a form of worship. Our strength is a big portion of our mind, body, and spirit balance for us to fulfill our purpose and be the most extraordinary version that we can be!

What Is Muscular Strength—and Why Does It Matter?

Muscular strength is the ability of your body to produce force—to overcome resistance and handle life's challenges physically, mentally, and spiritually. And here's the truth:

You don't get old and weak—You get weak, and then you get old.

If you don't train and stress your body through resistance and effort, it will break down. This is why strength is a cornerstone of the Extraordinary Strength Method™—because a strong body supports a strong mind and spirit, and gives you the ability to serve, move, and live your mission.

This is where so many people end up losing their quality of life the fastest. A strong body is a healthy body. Training your strength is one of the biggest aspects of living a healthy life. Everyone should strength-train. There is no age minimum or maximum because it is beneficial for all ages. Whether you are male or female, strength training is a must!

Strength Training Is for Everyone – No Excuses

There is so much confusion, and honestly crap, out there that dissuades people from making healthy decisions, and strength training seems to be one of those topics. No matter your age or fitness level, strength is for you.

For kids, it teaches them proper body mechanics and helps them learn to move well and through good ranges of motion. Some will say it will stunt their growth, and that isn't the case. The amount of force it would take for a growth plate to get broken while strength training is tremendous. Kids have a higher likelihood of stunting their growth from playing sports, and that doesn't happen often at all.

With that being said, kids should always be strength training with a certified professional, so teach them how to do it properly and safely as well as giving them the correct progressions and adjustments needed for them on an individual basis.

Now, for older populations, many worry about injuries and their own abilities while strength training. With the proper training program, strength training is life-saving. It will improve their body mechanics as well as range of motion so they are able to move better and more often.

Again, there should be a certified professional working with them to prescribe the proper movements and make adjustments as needed for each person. They do not need to be treated like babies and handed one pound weights. How is lifting a one pound weight going to make them stronger when their groceries weigh more than that? The muscle has to be stressed to get stronger and their movements in training should be based around the movements of their life, just as any other person training.

It's not about genes—it's about daily choices. Strength is built through consistent effort and the right coaching, no matter where you start.

Real Life Stories – The Extraordinary Strength Method™ in Action

A Three-Year-Old Miracle

I mentioned the three-year-old that I was training. She was brought to me by a friend and client of mine because she had been through a lot in her young life. She is her own miracle story. She had it hard right from the beginning.

She was stuck in the womb and not able to move, so after she was born, she had multiple surgeries before she was even one year old. Due to these complications and surgeries, she had a difficult time using her arms, hands, legs, and feet.

She was going through therapy but as she was turning three, they were removing the level of care she was receiving. That was when my friend approached me and asked me if I would be able to help. I absolutely wanted to do everything I could do.

Our goal was to focus on gaining strength and movement through her upper and lower body, really focusing on her lower body so she could walk up and down the stairs. Though we had to be focused and serious during certain parts of her training session, it still had to be built around some fun. Kids are kids, and they need to have fun in their activity, or it is just a chore.

I balanced games and training together, and over time she went from not being able to walk well to running around. From not being able to step up on a 45 pound bumper plate to going up and down the stairs with ease. From not being able to pick up 5 pounds, to picking up over 35 pounds. She is now five years old as I am writing this, and there isn't anything this wonderful little girl cannot do, and I am blessed to be a part of her story.

All of our training was basic movements, progressing over time to make it more challenging. This is why it can work for anyone.

My Grandparents

My grandparents are another great example at ages eighty-seven and eighty-five. They train to maintain quality of life and independence. We train basic movements to help them get stronger and continue to be functional throughout their day, from squats and deadlifts, to bench presses and pulldowns, the movements do not change much, because they are all part of what we do throughout each day.

Their strength is the key to their ability to maintain their quality of life because if they lose their strength, they lose their ability to walk around, do tasks around the house and the yard, and go on trips anywhere they want to go. When you lose strength and movement, you lose so much in your life, which can remove the ability to live out your purpose.

Lesson: Strength is for life—not just the gym.

Why Strength Training Matters (Extraordinary Strength Principles)

As well as all the above stated benefits, other benefits of muscular strength are increased muscle mass, improved metabolic rate, enhanced physical performance, and better bone density. The strength of your muscle is connected to the strength of your ligaments, the strength of your tendons, your bone density, your hormone health, and many other aspects of your health.

This is not to say you need to be an olympic lifter, but you should be relatively strong. No one wants to have someone else carry their groceries, take their laundry up and down the stairs, or not be able to get down on the ground and back up with their kids and grandkids.

Movement is crucial for longevity and improved quality of life, and if you do not have the strength to move and move well, the quality of life decreases. On the other hand, increased muscle leads to better movement, less joint and body pain, as well as burning more calories with more muscle mass. That means throughout the day you burn more calories just doing your normal activity, and then when you are intentional with your activity, whether it be strength training or metabolic training, you burn more calories!

The more you put in, the more you get out. Pretty much a great rule of life. Strength builds confidence, resilience, and the ability to handle life's battles.

The Mental and Spiritual Side of Strength—Overcoming Limits

Now, much of the above you may have heard before or you already know, but there is something more that I have seen and experienced throughout my years of strength training and training others: the ability to overcome challenges. Strength isn't just about the body—it trains the mind to break free from self-limiting beliefs.

Just like how high intensity and endurance training will help you become grittier, so will lifting heavy and working on getting stronger. I have watched people constantly choose the light weight, the easy weight, all because it is comfortable, and they know they can do it. When I tell them to go up, you can see it, and sometimes hear them say, "I don't think I can do it."

Thinking or saying this when they have not even tried it yet, and typically after I watched them nearly throw the previous weight around like it was a plastic bag. Then when urged to go up, and they do it, typically with ease, they are completely astounded and ecstatic that they could do it! With one simple lift, they learned they were more capable than they thought.

This is why in our Training for Warrior program, we train our students to work up to a one repetition max in certain lifts. A one rep max is how heavy someone can lift a weight for one rep and not be able to go up any higher.

Now, all of our students earn their exercises, meaning they must have proven they can do all the previous variations perfectly before moving up to our more complex lifts. Once they have trained that movement enough to perform it safely and effectively, then they get the opportunity to max out.

We max one complex lift each month, and it is my favorite day of the month. The energy and enthusiasm during those days is outrageous, and the celebrations and overcomes that happen are even more so. The first time someone does a max lift and realizes how strong they truly are is intoxicating for them and for everyone who is there! When someone is taking a max attempt, the entire class stops what they are doing and cheers them on, giving them everything they have so they can give everything they have. Nearly everyone has cried tears of joy during these days, for others and themselves.

Performing a max lift is stressful, though. Typically, it is a weight that has never been attempted and can bring on fear. In the beginning, most do not know how to use that fear to fuel them, and it can hinder their ability to perform the lift. They are stuck in their own head and self-limiting belief. They fear failure.

But, having amazing students and coaches around them, they take the attempt anyway and some succeed and complete the lift, while others do not complete it. Both are amazing results, though. Whether they complete the lift or not, taking on that challenge is a huge victory.

Truly, we want all of our students to fail, as I talked about before. This gives great feedback on the areas that need to be worked on and a true understanding of their strength. But overcoming the challenge and building that mental strength to take on the obstacle and challenge head on is what can truly change your life.

Doing these max lifts during strength training helps to build up that grit to take on the challenges of life. Proving to yourself in your training that you are stronger physically and mentally than you thought empowers you to push forward through life's challenges. Fear of failure holds most people back—in the gym and in life. But when you face a barbell, push past fear, and succeed (or fail and try again), you're training to face life's hardest moments with courage.

To get to that point, though, you need a lot of training first. As stated before, safety is first and a max attempt is something that is earned within our program and facility. There is a lot of training and intentionality that has to come before an attempt like that. This is where all of the strength really comes from.

The standard is 2–3 days per week of strength training. That means that 2–3 days per week, all you are focusing on is lifting. To gain strength, you must have an appropriate amount of weight to stress the body and muscles for them to grow stronger.

Strength training is not light weights for high repetitions, it is lower repetitions and heavier weight. To gain strength, you should be doing less than eight reps per set of the exercise you are doing. In the beginning, while learning the movement, it is good to have lighter weights and higher reps to learn to do the movement safely. You only learn with repetition.

Once the movement is being done well and safely, then you can work on increasing the weights and lowering the reps. The amount of sets you do will vary based on your ability, amount of time training, goals, and so on.

But without going too far down the rabbit hole, a great way to start is three to four sets of the movement and eight to ten reps per set. You do not want to overdo it. The goal for the first few weeks getting into strength training is learning how to do the movements properly and safely. If you go too hard too quickly, you will be extremely sore and not able to do much else for the next few days.

That is not a good thing. When your quality of life decreases due to your exercise, that is a bad thing. Soreness is not a good indicator of a good workout. A little soreness is okay, but it should not be so bad you have a hard time moving.

When something is new to the muscles or a higher intensity/usage than what it is used to, there will be a much higher breakdown of muscle, which will lead to higher soreness. We actually do not want that. When it takes long days to recover, you will not be gaining strength since you are losing movement and training time. It is better to take it slow when starting, to get your body used to the exercises before increasing the intensity of your strength training.

One more note, you do not need to confuse your muscles to see results. On the contrary, you need to be consistent with your strength training movements to see results. A strength program should run a minimum of four weeks. This is so we can build consistency in the movements and progress those movements.

We are looking for progressive overload, meaning that each week, after taking time to learn the movements, we are progressing either in weight, reps, or sets that we are doing of that particular movement. A little upon a little builds a lot, and consistency is key. If you are not sure where to start, have a professional help you. As Martin Rooney says, "*Everyone needs a Coach!*"

Spiritual Strength: Lifting Beyond the Gym

Muscular strength has to also correlate into your spiritual strength and faith. Strength in faith is often built through overcoming challenges and adversities as well. Just as lifting weights increases muscular strength, facing and overcoming spiritual challenges strengthens one's faith and trust in Christ.

There are those times in your life when there is nowhere to turn and fear starts to take its hold on you. Not sure if you are going to be able to keep going. Not sure if you have what it takes. This is where your strength is tested in your faith and trust in Jesus.

> *"Trust in the Lord with all your heart, and do not lean on your own understanding. In all your ways acknowledge him, and he will make straight your paths." – Proverbs 3:5-6 (ESV)*

This is true strength in faith. Trusting in God when there seems to be no hope. He is the hope. He is our strength. You build strength in your faith by trusting in God and overcoming obstacles.

Strength in faith is not sitting around waiting for God to just make things better for you, it is praying to God and asking for the strength and the discernment of His will for you so you can take action on what He says to do.

Obedience is the strength of faith.

Persisting through the obstacle to obey what God has called you to do is the strength of faith.

God never said life would be easy, He told us to take up your cross and follow Him. We are going to have good and bad times, but God is our strength through it all.

> *"I know how to be brought low, and I know how to abound. In any and every circumstance, I have learned the secret of facing plenty and hunger, abundance and need. I can do all things through Him who strengthens me." – Philippians 4:12-13 (ESV)*

Our true strength comes from Christ, and just like training your body to be strong, you must train your faith to be strong. This means building that relationship with Christ through prayer, reading His word, trusting in Him in every area of our lives, and giving every area of our life over to Him. When things are going good or become hard, we must always rely on Him and give over our lives to Him. Honor God by training your body and keeping it strong and healthy so you may fulfill your purpose and realize that true strength comes from the Lord.

As muscles grow under pressure, faith grows under challenge. Training for strength—both physically and spiritually—prepares you to walk boldly into the purpose God has for you. It's important to challenge self-limiting beliefs and push beyond comfort zones to develop strength both physically and spiritually.

Spiritual strength, like physical strength, grows through perseverance and trust in God, particularly in times of adversity. Faith strength is built by obeying God when it's hard, trusting Him when you can't see the way, and persevering when life feels heavy.

Key Benefits of Strength Training (The Extraordinary Strength Method™):

- Increased muscle mass and improved physical performance

- Enhanced metabolic rate and bone density

- Strengthens ligaments, tendons, and joints

- Enables functional movement, reducing risk of injury and improving quality of life

- Improved mental toughness, discipline, and confidence

- Spiritual resilience—faith strengthened through adversity and perseverance

Reflection Questions – Building Strength for Purpose:

- What self-limiting beliefs have held you back from building physical or spiritual strength?

- How can you apply progressive overload to your faith (praying longer, deeper trust, harder obedience)?

- What does functional strength look like in your daily life? Carrying groceries, playing with kids, serving others?

- How can trusting in God's strength help you overcome personal or physical challenges?

- Are you treating your body as a living sacrifice for God's purpose? (Romans 12:1)

By training both physical and spiritual strength consistently, you honor God and become equipped to handle life's challenges with resilience and perseverance. This physical and spiritual strength will lead you to becoming that extraordinary you God plans on you being!

Habits to Build:
Strength the Extraordinary Strength Way

- Train for Strength with Purpose
  - Schedule 2–3 days per week for strength training focused on compound resistance movements.
  - Start with form and technique—safety is the first priority before increasing weight.

- Apply Progressive Overload
  - Build strength by slowly increasing weight, reps, or sets.
  - Use 3–4 sets of 8–10 reps as a starting point and progress with intention.

- Build Strength at Every Age
  - Kids, seniors, and adults can all train for strength safely with proper coaching.
  - Choose real-life movements that enhance daily function and mobility.

- Train Mind and Spirit with the Body
  - Challenge mental limits by pushing beyond your comfort zone.

- Reflect on Scripture or pray before/during training to unite physical discipline with spiritual growth.
- Stay Consistent and Committed
    - Follow a structured program for at least four weeks to create lasting change.
    - Avoid chasing soreness—aim for steady progress over intensity spikes.
- Train for Life, Not Just Aesthetics
    - Choose exercises that improve your ability to live actively and serve others.
    - View strength as a preparation tool for your God-given purpose.
- Lift for Spiritual Growth
    - Use your training time to lean on God's strength when fear or fatigue sets in.
    - Let each lift become a symbol of trust, obedience, and perseverance.

Bring It Together: Strength in Action

- Honor God with your body.
    - Let your training become a living sacrifice—train with purpose, not vanity. (Romans 12:1)
- Push through fear.
    - Step up to the barbell and your challenges even when doubt creeps in—trust God's strength over your own.
- Choose functional over flashy.

- Train for life—lift so you can serve, move well, and maintain independence for the long haul.

- Pair strength training with prayer.
  - Reflect on Scripture or pray before lifting—strengthen your faith while strengthening your body.

- Celebrate every win—big or small.
  - Whether it's lifting a new weight or simply showing up, acknowledge your progress and God's provision.

- Lead by example.
  - Show others what strength in faith looks like through how you live, serve, and persevere.

- Let your struggles build resilience.
  - Physical strength grows through resistance—so does faith. Embrace the challenge and lean on God.

- Train as an act of worship.
  - Every rep, every workout, every act of discipline is a chance to give glory to God.

Final Charge: Strength is the Foundation of the Extraordinary You

Strength—physical, mental, and spiritual—empowers you to live out your God-given purpose. Without strength, you won't have the capacity to serve, love, and lead as God calls you to.

"Be strong and courageous. Do not be afraid; do not be discouraged, for the Lord your God will be with you wherever you go." — Joshua 1:9 (NIV)

Through The Extraordinary Strength Method™, strength becomes your weapon against fear, your platform for serving others, and your path to becoming the extraordinary you.

Whether you are starting with a single push-up or preparing for your next personal record, your training becomes a living sacrifice (Romans 12:1)—a bold act of worship that says, *"Lord, I will honor You with this body, this moment, and this strength."*

Let your training speak.

Let your strength serve.

Let your faith grow stronger under pressure.

And let your life be the evidence of the extraordinary strength that comes from God alone.

Strong in body. Strong in mind. Strong in faith. Strong for your purpose.

Recap: Pillar 1 — Training: Building Strength for Life and Purpose (Extraordinary Strength in Action)

As we've walked through this first pillar of The Extraordinary Strength Method™, one thing is clear—training your body is not optional if you want to live out your God-given purpose. It's a calling. A responsibility. An act of worship.

Your body is the house of your mind and spirit—and without a strong body, you can't carry out the mission God has for your life. This is why Training is the foundation that supports everything else—your mind, spirit, and purpose.

Let's recap what we've learned and how to put it into action:

Part 1: Training – The Foundation of Extraordinary Strength for Everyone

- Training is for everyone—no matter your age, gender, or current level. Whether you're three or ninety-four, training keeps you strong, independent, and ready for life.

- Your body is the temple of the Holy Spirit (1 Corinthians 6:19-20). Taking care of it is a way to honor God and worship Him with your life.

- A weak body limits your purpose. A strong body unlocks the ability to serve God, serve others, and fulfill your mission.

- Training is more than just fitness—it's about building strength for life. Strength to serve, lead, and persevere.

- Extraordinary strength begins here—because it takes physical, mental, and spiritual strength to stand firm in life's battles.

Part 2: Cardiovascular Endurance – Building Physical and Spiritual Grit

- The Extraordinary Strength Method™ trains both body and mind through endurance work—pushing limits in training builds the grit you need for life.

- Endurance is a mental and spiritual challenge, as much as a physical one. Most people give up in their mind before their body is done. That's why endurance training builds grit, perseverance, and faith.

- Cardiovascular endurance strengthens the heart, lungs, and mind—but also trains your spirit to endure hardship, trials, and the race God has called you to run.

- Through interval training, metabolic circuits, or intentional endurance work, you not only build stamina but train your mind to overcome self-limiting beliefs.

- Spiritually, endurance mirrors the faith journey—sticking close to God through prayer, scripture, and trust when life gets hard (James 1:2-4, Romans 5:3-4).

- Endurance reminds us that strength doesn't come from staying comfortable—but from pushing beyond what you think you can do.

- Mental barriers will rise—but The Extraordinary Strength Method™ teaches you to push beyond them and grow stronger physically and spiritually.

Part 3: Muscular Strength – Building the Power to Serve and Persevere

- Strength is a command from God. *"Love the Lord your God with all your heart, soul, and strength."* – Mark 12:30 (NIV)

- You don't get old and then weak—you get weak, and then old. Training your muscles fights aging, atrophy, and loss of independence.

- Strength training is for everyone—men, women, young, old—and it's the key to keeping your body capable of life, family, and calling.

- The Extraordinary Strength Method™ uses progressive strength training to help you overcome self-limiting beliefs—because strength training teaches you that you are more capable than you think.

- Strength training is about more than physical muscle—it's about building mental toughness, overcoming fear, and destroying self-limiting beliefs.

- Stories of breakthrough: You've read about the three-year-old girl who gained strength to overcome her limitations and the eighty-seven-year-old grandparents who are still active and independent—all because they trained for strength.

- In the same way, spiritual strength is developed by trusting God through adversity, leaning on His power, and persevering in faith when life gets hard. (Philippians 4:13, Proverbs 3:5-6)

- You learned that strength training is a lifelong practice—just like following Jesus. Both require discipline, perseverance, and a willingness to face challenges head-on.

Extraordinary Strength Method™ Mindset Recap: What You Learned About Yourself

- You're stronger than you think. You can overcome physical, mental, and spiritual obstacles.

- Your body is a tool for purpose, not vanity. You train to serve and glorify God.

- Endurance and strength are built one rep, one step, one prayer at a time. It's a process of daily obedience and discipline.

- Discomfort is growth. You can push past mental and physical limits—and you should.

- Strength and faith are connected. As you grow in one, you grow in the other.

- Consistency is key. Extraordinary strength is built by showing up and doing the work—day after day.

Core Lessons from Pillar 1 (The Extraordinary Strength Method™ in Action)

1. Training is Worship — Caring for your body is a way to glorify God and prepare for His calling.

2. Strength is a Responsibility — You need strength to fulfill your purpose and serve others well.

3. Endurance Builds Perseverance — Cardiovascular training develops perseverance for life's challenges—mentally, physically, and spiritually.

4. Strength Overcomes Fear — Muscular strength teaches you to break self-limiting beliefs and face life with resilience.

5. Mind-Body-Spirit Connection — All training—whether for endurance or strength—is a spiritual discipline that builds trust in God.

6. Small Actions, Big Results — Extraordinary strength comes from small, consistent choices stacked over time.

Extraordinary Strength Action Steps—Put Training into Practice

- Daily Movement: Strive for 10,000 steps a day—movement is life.

- Strength Training: 2–3 days a week of resistance training to build and maintain muscle.

- Cardiovascular Endurance: 1–3 days a week of interval or endurance training to build stamina and heart health.

- Push Mental Barriers: Every workout, challenge self-limiting beliefs. Do something harder than last time.

- Spiritual Training: Just like your body, train your spirit daily through prayer, Bible reading, and trust in God.

- Consistency: Stay the course. Strength—physical and spiritual—is built over time, not overnight.

Reflection Questions: How Are You Training for Extraordinary Strength?

- Am I treating my body as a living sacrifice to God? (Romans 12:1)

- What fears or self-limiting beliefs are keeping me weak—both in training and in life?

- How can I align my fitness journey with my faith journey?

- Am I prepared—mentally, physically, and spiritually—to carry out the purpose God has for me?

- What training habit can I start today to become stronger for my purpose?

- Where do I need to apply endurance or strength spiritually—where have I been giving up too soon?

What's Next: Pillar 2 — Nutrition (Fuel for Strength and Purpose)

Now that you understand how to train your body to be strong for life and purpose, we move to fueling your body for that mission.

Because no matter how strong you get in the gym—if you don't fuel your body right, it will eventually fail you. Your training will be limited if you're not eating in a way that supports strength, endurance, and purpose.

And even more importantly—nutrition is another way to honor God with your body.

So up next, we'll dive into:

- How to honor God with what you put in your body.
- How to balance discipline and flexibility in nutrition.
- How to fuel for energy, purpose, and longevity—not just for looks.
- And how food, discipline, and faith are deeply connected in living an extraordinary life.

You've laid the foundation. You've built the beginning of extraordinary strength. Now let's fuel that strength for life, purpose, and glory to God. Get ready. You're just getting started on your path to becoming the extraordinary you. Let's go!

Pillar 2: Nutrition – Fueling the Temple for Purpose and Power

"It is written, 'Man shall not live by bread
alone, but by every word that comes from the
mouth of God.'" – Matthew 4:4 (ESV)

If strength training is how we build the body, then nutrition is how we fuel it. Just as the mind requires discipline and the spirit requires faith, the body requires nourishment—intentional, consistent, and aligned with our purpose. You can train daily, have impeccable discipline, and still fall short if what you're putting into your body is tearing it down.

This is where the Extraordinary Strength Method™ brings clarity. In every cornerstone of mind, body, and spirit, there are pillars that support your God-given greatness. Nutrition is one of the most critical pillars of the Body Cornerstone. You can't become the extraordinary version of yourself if you neglect what fuels the temple God has entrusted you to steward.

Understand that society has misused the word diet and the word spirit and gave these words a completely different meaning. We will talk about spirit later, but as for the word diet, it is defined as "the kinds of food that a person habitually eats." The key word here is habitually. We live in a world where the word "diet" has been twisted into temporary restrictions and shame-based approaches. Your 'diet' is what you eat normally. It is not a thirty-day shred or detox where you are insanely restrictive for that time and then go right back to what you were doing beforehand. Just like spiritual strength is not built in one church service or one prayer, physical health isn't built on a single perfect week of eating. It's what you repeat that determines who you become.

So for you to change your body and diet, it takes changing habits and lifestyle, not something short term. This is something that every person has control over. Training can go through seasons depending on where you are at in your life, meaning that during some times in your life you may be able to train four days per week for at least an hour at a time, whereas other times in your life you may only get two intentional days per week. It's not the end of the world, it happens. But the one thing you have complete control over is what you put into your mouth. Sure, there are times when you do not get the choice of what to eat, like at a gathering of some sort, but you can control how much you eat and drink there. No matter what is going on in your life, it is always your choice and your responsibility.

That's part of spiritual maturity: choosing stewardship over convenience. Whether you're at a celebration, under stress, or surrounded by temptation, your response reveals your discipline—and discipline is a fruit of both physical training and spiritual growth.

Fueling the Temple

Repeating the verses from 1 Corinthians 6:19-20 (NIV): "*Do you not know that your bodies are temples of the Holy Spirit, who is in you, whom you have received from God? You are not your own; you were bought at a price. Therefore honor God with your bodies.*"

This verse isn't just spiritual—it's extremely practical. We are supposed to be treating our bodies with respect and care. Eating healthy is a way to honor the body as a temple of the Holy Spirit. When we eat and drink junk, we are dishonoring our bodies that God gave to us and also dishonoring God as well. Our bodies should be treated well, which means we need to fuel it with the right foods and drinks.

I always teach it as if you are putting fuel into your car. If you drive a gas vehicle, you wouldn't put diesel in it because you know it would destroy it. Our bodies are no different, other than it takes longer for our bodies to be destroyed by the "diesel" that is put into it. So many want their body to be working at peak performance while putting the wrong fuel into it. It is hard for your body to function the way it should, especially for great performance, if it is not being taken care of and fueled properly. Your body is far more valuable—eternal purpose lives within it. Treat it that way. Honor yourself and our Lord by treating your body to the right fuel, the right nutrition, and see how well you are able to perform each day.

The Extraordinary Strength Method™ teaches that your physical inputs impact spiritual output. When your body is strong and fueled, your mind is clearer, your spirit more aligned, and your service to others more sustainable.

Proverbs 23:20-21(NIV) says *"Do not join those who drink too much wine or gorge themselves on meat, for drunkards and gluttons become poor, and drowsiness clothes them in rags."*

The Bible warns against gluttony and excess, encouraging moderation in eating. It says that overeating or indulging in unhealthy food can lead to physical and spiritual consequences. Overeating and drinking is a major issue in our society. Hence, why the overweight and obesity percentage is over 73 percent in the United States.

Portion control and not over indulging can change everything. Eating well does not mean you cannot have some of the "fun" stuff. The problem is most people eat more of the "fun" stuff than they do of the right stuff. From TFW, we use the 80/20 rule. 80 percent of your calorie intake and what you eat and drink should be the right stuff. 20 percent of your calorie intake and what you eat and drink is the room for the fun stuff.

I do not need to take any time explaining what the right stuff is because everyone knows. If I tested you on what was the right choice with comparisons of food, you would likely get 100 percent on the test. The problem is not that people do not know what to eat, they just don't do what they know and fall prey to quick gratification and convenience over the right choice.

A very simple way to not overindulge is by hand measurements. Every meal should have a palm size of protein, no more than a thumb size of fat, a fist size of vegetables, and a fist size of carbs. If every meal you ate is portioned like this, there is no room for overindulging, and it will be very well-balanced!

Genesis 1:29 (NIV) says, "*Then God said, 'I give you every seed-bearing plant on the face of the whole earth and every tree that has fruit with seed in it. They will be yours for food.'*"

This verse highlights that God provided plant-based foods for nourishment for us. It underscores the value of natural, whole foods as part of a healthy diet. God did not intend on us having ultra-processed foods within our diet.

Another great and simple tool from TFW is the concept that if it came from a plant, you can eat it. If it came from within a plant, don't. This means that if it is natural whole food that is not made by people inside a plant, that is the food choice you should be eating. Again, this is simple, but knowing what to do versus actually doing it is where the major issue is.

Discipline isn't a knowledge issue. It's a follow-through issue. That's why training your spirit alongside your nutrition habits is key. It builds self-control, obedience, and gratitude.

Mindfulness & Gratitude in Eating

1 Timothy 4:4-5 (ESV) says: "*For everything created by God is good, and nothing is to be rejected if it is received with thanksgiving, for it is made holy by the word of God and prayer.*"

This passage encourages gratitude for the food provided and implies that food should be consumed with mindfulness and thankfulness, aligning with a moderate and healthy approach to eating.

Mindless eating gets so many people into trouble with their nutrition. Sitting on the couch with an entire bag of chips is never going to end well for most people. Before you know it, the bag is completely empty and you have no idea how you ate all of it. Your mind was enveloped in whatever you were watching and without thinking, you just kept eating and eating.

Mindfulness while eating can make a huge change in your life. This doesn't just mean when you are watching TV, it is with nearly everything. What I mean is that if you choose to eat mindfully, you have to consider all aspects of when you choose to eat. Do you eat when you are happy or celebrating? How about when you are sad? Stressed? Anxious or depressed? How about when you are hanging out with friends or family?

Understanding what triggers you to eat or how you eat is true dietary mindfulness. It first starts with making yourself aware of those things and then being mindful during those times. Have a plan in place to keep yourself mindful while hanging out with other people and when celebrating. If emotional eating is an issue, do something that will captivate your mind better, whether it is reading, writing, going for a walk or working out. There are so many great choices but the only way to change that habit is by making yourself aware and mindful and then taking different actions. The enemy works subtly through comfort, distraction, and emotional cravings. But mindfulness and gratitude interrupt that cycle.

The other piece of this is thankfulness for our food. Many do not think of how most of us have nearly unlimited access to food. Not everyone in the world has that, especially healthy, clean food. Showing gratitude and thankfulness for all that we have from God is a great way to stay mindful.

Romans 14:20-21(NIV) says, "*Do not destroy the work of God for the sake of food. All food is clean, but it is wrong for a person to eat anything that causes someone else to stumble. It is better not to eat meat or drink wine, or to do anything else that will cause your brother or sister to fall.*"

While this passage is more about considering others' spiritual well-being, it reflects the principle of mindfulness in eating—considering the impact of our choices on ourselves and others. It also reflects the aspect from above that we do not want to destroy what God's purpose is for us for the sake of food.

I see it this way:

1) You should not destroy your body just because something tastes great and overindulge just for the sake of eating.

2) You should not make others stumble by tempting them or making them feel bad because they are not overindulging with you.

This second point happens so often and I see it all the time with our students. They are out with friends and are making better food choices, and then their so-called friends start trying to make them feel bad that they are not eating and drinking as they are. This frustrates me because they are trying to drag that person into their own bad choices. If they want to treat their bodies like crap, that is their choice, and others should not be made to feel guilty that they are not doing the same thing. I talked about it before, but if this is how your friends treat you, it is time to get new friends.

Along the same lines, some will bring unhealthy food or snacks around as a celebration. If you know that someone is trying to eat and be healthier, do not tempt them with unhealthy choices. No one is that strong that they can always deny those things. You wouldn't offer someone who became sober a drink, at least I hope not, so don't tempt those that are trying to change their health. Be mindful for yourself and for others. Encourage them. Celebrate their discipline. Choose to be someone who builds up, not one who pulls others down.

The Bible encourages us to have a balanced approach to eating that emphasizes moderation, gratitude, mindfulness, and the consumption of wholesome, natural foods. By honoring your body as a temple, practicing self-control, and being mindful of your food choices, you align with biblical principles that promote physical, mental, and spiritual well-being that will help you to become the extraordinary version of yourself and fulfill God's purpose for your life.

Your body is a temple of the Holy Spirit, and it is your responsibility to honor it through proper nutrition, self-control, and balanced living. Your diet is a long-term lifestyle, not a quick fix. This also aligns with spiritual well-being—just as you need to feed your body with the right fuel, you need to nourish your spirit with the Word of God.

Reflection Questions

- How are you honoring God with your food choices?

- What small change can you make this week to improve your nutrition?

- How does your current diet reflect discipline, gratitude, and purpose?

- What triggers cause you to overeat or make poor food choices (stress, emotion, boredom, etc.)?

- Are you treating your body as a living sacrifice and temple of the Holy Spirit, or as an afterthought?

- In what ways can you build a more mindful and prayerful relationship with food?

- Who or what environments cause you to stumble with your nutrition choices—and how can you create healthier boundaries or accountability?

- How can your approach to eating reflect your long-term purpose, not just short-term satisfaction?

Habits to Build: Nutrition for the Temple

- Follow the 80/20 Principle
    - Make 80% of your diet whole, God-made foods, and allow 20% for flexibility. This creates sustainability, not shame.

- Use Hand Measurements for Portion Control
    - A palm of protein, fist of carbs and vegetables, and thumb of fat helps create balanced, non-restrictive meals.

- Practice Mindful Eating
    - Pause before meals. Ask yourself: Why am I eating? Am I stressed, emotional, or truly hungry?

- Eat with Gratitude
    - Pray before meals. Give thanks for the provision, and treat your body as the temple God gave you.

- Plan Ahead and Stay Accountable
    - Prep meals weekly. Track how nutrition affects your energy, mindset, and faith. Work with a coach or accountability group.

Bring It Together: Fueling with Purpose In Action

- Plan your meals for the week on Sunday. Include at least 3 meals a day made from whole foods.

- Commit to praying before every meal for the next 7 days to build mindfulness and gratitude.

- Identify one habit trigger (stress, emotion, social pressure) and create a replacement plan to respond differently.

- Apply the 80/20 rule at your next social event—make the best choice you can without guilt.

- Journal your food choices and how they made you feel—physically and spiritually—for three days.

- Remove one ultra-processed item from your pantry and replace it with a whole food.

- Encourage a family member or friend to join you in a nutrition habit shift—build community and accountability.

By making small, consistent changes to your nutrition and maintaining spiritual mindfulness, you'll honor your body as a temple, promoting overall well-being, and aligning with God's purpose for your life and becoming the extraordinary you.

Final Charge: From Fueling the Temple to Shaping It

Your nutrition is a spiritual issue just as much as it's a physical one. In the Extraordinary Strength Method™, you are called to fuel your temple, not just for performance, but for purpose. Your body is not your own—it is a vessel of the Holy Spirit. By nourishing it with discipline and gratitude, you'll not only feel better and live longer—you'll align more fully with God's plan for your life.

Don't wait for a perfect Monday to start. Start with your next meal. One choice at a time. Because every bite you take can either bring you closer to your purpose—or further from it.

You were created for more. Fuel like it.

When you combine intentional training with disciplined nutrition, something powerful happens—your body begins to transform. Not just in how it looks, but in how it moves, performs, and endures. And more importantly, in how it serves.

Nutrition lays the foundation. It's the daily stewardship of what you allow into your body. Training builds the structure—it's how you challenge your body to grow stronger and more capable. But body composition is the reflection of those efforts. It's the physical outcome of your internal choices—both physically and spiritually.

In the Extraordinary Strength Method™, Body Composition is the third pillar of the Body Cornerstone. It's not about chasing a number on a scale. It's about honoring the body God gave you by developing a body that is strong, lean, energized, and ready to carry out the mission He's placed on your life.

So now that we've laid the groundwork through training and nutrition, let's take a deeper look into what body composition really means, how it impacts your health and faith, and how it can be a tool—not a trap—for fulfilling your purpose and becoming the extraordinary version of you.

Let's dive into Pillar 3.

Pillar 3: Body Composition – Reflecting Strength, Stewardship, and Purpose.

"Dear friend, I pray that you may enjoy good health and that all may go well with you, even as your soul is getting along well." — 3 John 1:2 (NIV)

Your body composition—the balance between fat and muscle—does more than shape how you look. It affects how you live. It influences your energy, longevity, health risks, and most importantly, your ability to fulfill the purpose God created you for. This is not about chasing aesthetics; it's about stewardship. About honoring the body God gave you so you can live fully, love deeply, and serve purposefully.

In the Extraordinary Strength Method™, Body Composition is the final pillar of the Body Cornerstone—built on a foundation of Training and Nutrition. It's the result of your daily decisions in both the physical and spiritual disciplines. This pillar reflects the visible fruit of invisible faith and consistent action.

Yes, this is where we get into body fat. I know for some this may be a touchy subject, but to live the extraordinary life that God has called you to, you cannot let your body composition end your life early. We honor God by honoring our bodies and taking care of it, so it should be a priority in life. No, I will not be telling you that you need to be a certain weight, but, I am going to tell you that you should have a certain body fat percentage to live a healthy life. Let's dive into some information first, though.

Understanding Body Composition

Body composition is the ratio of fat to lean tissue (muscles, bones, organs, etc.) in the body. This is typically measured by percent body fat, which is the percentage amount of a person's total weight in fat. So if someone has 33 percent body fat, that means that one third of their weight is fat. The higher the percent body fat, the higher risk for disease and a lot of health issues. We use this measuring system in our gym because it gives us a better picture of someone's body health over just their weight alone.

BMI (Body Mass Index) does not give us a good picture since it is only a height and weight analysis. It does not take into consideration someone's fat or muscle, just the total weight. For example, someone can appear "overweight" on the scale or BMI chart but be lean, muscular, and metabolically healthy. On the flip side, someone can be "skinny" but have high body fat and be at high risk for disease. It's not about the number on the scale—it's about what that number is made of.

I've experienced this firsthand. I am 5'10" and weigh around 210 pounds. BMI calculation puts me at 30.1 which is considered obese. Well, by that standard, I need to lose a lot of weight. But, if we look at my body composition and body fat percentage, it tells a different story. My body fat percentage is around 10 percent which is in the "athletes" category of one of the body fat percent charts. So where is the major issue? BMI does not consider muscle mass at all. I have higher muscle mass which is why my weight is higher, not because I have too much fat. This is why body composition is important to understand the bigger picture of a person's health. BMI can create a lot of issues when people are only focused on the number on the scale instead of what their body is composed of. This is why we emphasize body composition—not just weight—at our gym and within the Extraordinary Strength Method™.

Below is a body fat percent chart from the American Council on Exercise.

BUILTLEAN®		
ACE Body Fat Chart		
Description	Men	Women
Essential fat	2-5%	10-13%
Athletes	6-13%	14-20%
Fitness	14-17%	21-24%
Average	18-24%	25-31%
Obese	25%+	32%+

These percentages may vary slightly with age, but the key point is clear: excess body fat increases your health risks significantly.

Why It Matters for Your Purpose

So why is it important to have a healthy body fat percentage? Well, the risks that are involved with high body fat should answer that.

The National Institute of Health lists out these risks for those that are overweight and obese:

- Type 2 diabetes
- High blood pressure
- Heart disease
- Stroke
- Metabolic syndrome
- Fatty liver diseases
- Some cancers
- Breathing problems
- Sleep disorders
- Osteoarthritis
- Gout
- Diseases of the gallbladder and pancreas
- Kidney disease
- Pregnancy problems
- Fertility problems
- Sexual function problems
- Mental health problems

So many of these things are preventable by taking care of your health and having a proper body composition. Many die from these things. This is why your body composition is important for you to be the most extraordinary you and to fulfill your purpose. If you don't take time to take care of your health, there will come a time when you will have no choice and you will wish you would have done something about it beforehand.

We are on this earth to serve others, but we are not able to do that if we are too unhealthy to do so. Taking care of your health is part of the spiritual balance that will lead you to the extraordinary, because if your health fails, you no longer get the ability to do it.

The Spiritual Parallel: Composed for Purpose

Just as your physical body has a composition, so does your spiritual life. A healthy spirit isn't built overnight, and it doesn't thrive on convenience. Like the physical body, your spirit needs balance, intentionality, and nourishment.

A balanced spiritual life involves maintaining a healthy "composition" of practices, beliefs, and values. Just as a balanced body composition supports overall health, a balanced spiritual life supports well-being and fulfillment. Maintaining a healthy body composition through a balanced diet and exercise parallels maintaining a balanced spiritual life through a mix of worship, spending time in God's word, serving others, prayer, and personal reflection.

This verse is worth repeating, just from another translation. "*Beloved, I pray that all may go well with you and that you may be in good health, as it goes well with your soul.*" – 3 John 1:2 (ESV)

Your mind, body, and spirit are always better when in good health. You need that healthy composition and balance to be the extraordinary you that you are capable of. If your spirit has bad composition, just like if your body has bad composition, there are many risks involved in that:

1) Emotional and Mental Health Risks

   a) Increased Stress and Anxiety: Without a spiritual foundation to provide perspective and solace, stress and anxiety can become overwhelming.

   b) Depression: A lack of spiritual fulfillment can contribute to feelings of emptiness and depression.

   c) Loss of Purpose: Without spiritual direction, you might struggle to find meaning and purpose in your life, leading to feelings of aimlessness and dissatisfaction.

   d) Poor Coping Mechanisms: Spiritual practices often provide healthy coping mechanisms for life's challenges. Without them, individuals may resort to unhealthy behaviors such as substance abuse or overeating.

2) Physical Health Risks

   a) Weakened Immune System: Chronic stress and emotional distress, often alleviated through spiritual practices, can weaken the immune system, making one more susceptible to illnesses.

   b) Poor Sleep Quality: Lack of spiritual peace can lead to insomnia or poor sleep quality, affecting overall health and functioning.

   c) High Blood Pressure and Heart Disease: The stress and anxiety from a lack of spiritual balance can increase the risk of hypertension and cardiovascular diseases.

3) Relationship and Social Risks

   a) Strained Relationships: A lack of spiritual grounding can affect how you interact with others, leading to strained relationships with family, friends, and colleagues.

   b) Social Isolation: Spiritual communities provide social support and a sense of belonging. Without this, individuals may experience social isolation and loneliness.

   c) Poor Communication Skills: The Bible emphasizes empathy, compassion, and active listening. Without these, communication in relationships can suffer.

4) Personal Development Risks

   a) Stagnation: Spiritual growth encourages personal development and self-improvement. Without it, you may feel stuck or stagnant in your personal growth.

   b) Lack of Resilience: Spiritual practices build resilience and the ability to bounce back from adversity. Without this, you may struggle to cope with challenges and setbacks.

5) Ethical and Moral Risks

   a) Compromised Values: A life following Jesus provides a moral and ethical framework. Without this, you will find it harder to navigate moral dilemmas and maintain integrity.

b) Increased Temptations: Without spiritual guidance, you are more prone to succumb to unhealthy or unethical temptations.

6) Existential Risks

a) Fear of Death and the Unknown: Spiritual beliefs often provide comfort regarding the afterlife or the meaning of existence. Without this, you could experience heightened fear and anxiety about death and the unknown.

b) Existential Crisis: A lack of spiritual grounding can lead to existential crises, where you question the meaning and purpose of life, leading to profound emotional distress.

7) Mitigating These Risks

a) Engage in Regular Spiritual Practices: Activities such as prayer, meditation, and reading the Bible provide a sense of peace and purpose.

b) Join a Spiritual Community (Church, Life Group, etc.): Being part of a community provides social support, accountability, and a sense of belonging.

c) Seek Guidance: Spiritual mentors, pastors, counselors, or leaders can provide support and guidance in navigating spiritual and life challenges.

d) Reflect and Journal: Regular self-reflection and journaling can help clarify beliefs, values, and goals, promoting a balanced spiritual life.

e) Balance with Physical and Mental Health: Ensure that your spiritual practices complement physical exercise and mental wellness activities for a balanced composition approach to well-being.

To have that healthy composition, by maintaining a balanced nutritional and spiritual life, you can enhance your emotional, mental, physical, social, and existential well-being, leading to a more fulfilled and meaningful life, becoming that extraordinary you God has called you to be!

Just like neglecting physical health leads to breakdown, neglecting spiritual practices leads to burnout. But when you invest in both—when you take care of your body and feed your soul—you experience a life of extraordinary strength and extraordinary peace.

That's the heart of this pillar: Balanced composition. Stewarded strength. Lasting purpose.

Body Fat and Faith: Honoring God Through Wholeness

As you can see, prioritizing the health of your body has an immense impact on your physical, mental, emotional, and spiritual well-being. If you do not prioritize the health of your body, the risks can be tremendous and the fulfilling and purposeful life that God has called you to live will slip out of your reach. You have greatness inside of you, but you have to control your controllables.

To live the extraordinary life God has called you to, you must honor Him by taking care of your body. A healthy body composition not only reduces physical health risks but also supports mental, emotional, and spiritual well-being. Neglecting your health can lead to preventable illnesses, reduced purpose, and spiritual imbalance. By maintaining a balanced composition of physical health, spiritual practices, and emotional resilience, you can become the extraordinary person you were created to be.

The Extraordinary Strength Method™ doesn't ask you to be shredded or perfect. It calls you to be intentional and faithful. To develop a body capable of carrying out God's work, and a spirit that stays strong in the storm.

Reflection Questions

- How has focusing solely on weight affected your health or confidence?

- How can shifting your focus to *body composition* change your mindset?

- In what ways does a healthy body allow you to better serve your purpose?

- How can you mirror physical balance in your spiritual life?

- What is one step you can take this week to improve your overall composition—physically or spiritually?

Habits to Build: Strengthening Your Composition

1. Prioritize Healthy Body Composition

- Focus on body fat percentage and lean muscle, not just weight.

2. Fuel Your Body for Performance

- Fuel your body with nutrient-dense foods that align with your health and spiritual goals.

3. Incorporate Regular Exercise

- Use exercise as a tool for both physical and spiritual growth.

4. Mitigate Health Risks with Preventative Habits

- Proactively address health risks linked to high body fat through preventive measures.

5. Strengthen Your Spiritual Foundation

- Build a spiritual life that supports your physical health and overall well-being.

6. Develop Emotional and Mental Resilience

- Maintain balance in mental and emotional health alongside physical and spiritual growth.

7. Find Accountability and Community

- Surround yourself with like-minded individuals for encouragement and support.

8. Track Progress Holistically

- Measure health through more than just numbers.

Bring It Together: Whole-Person Health In Action

1. Prioritize Healthy Body Composition

- Schedule regular body composition assessments (e.g., calipers, InBody, DEXA).
- Set realistic body fat goals that align with your age, gender, and activity level.
- Avoid scale obsession—track progress through strength, energy, and endurance.

2. Fuel Your Body for Performance

- Follow the 80/20 rule: Make 80 percent of your meals whole, nutrient-dense foods, allowing for 20 percent flexibility.
- Plan weekly meals that incorporate lean proteins, healthy fats, complex carbohydrates, and fresh produce.
- Practice gratitude before meals, reflecting on God's provision for your body's nourishment.

3. Incorporate Regular Exercise

- Commit to strength training 2–3 times per week to build lean muscle and improve body composition.
- Add 2–3 days of cardiovascular activities (walking, cycling, running) for heart health and endurance.
- Use workout time for reflection or prayer, focusing on gratitude for your body's abilities.

4. Mitigate Health Risks with Preventative Habits

- Schedule regular health screenings to monitor blood pressure, cholesterol, and glucose levels.

- Manage stress with relaxation techniques like deep breathing, yoga, or faith-based meditation.

- Establish a sleep routine, aiming for 7–9 hours per night to aid in recovery and weight management.

5. Strengthen Your Spiritual Foundation

- Develop daily spiritual practices, including prayer, Bible study, and worship.

- Serve others through community outreach, church activities, or just someone in need to enhance purpose and connection.

- Reflect weekly on your spiritual growth and how it impacts your health.

6. Develop Emotional and Mental Resilience

- Use journaling to process emotions, reflect on progress, write out prayers, and maintain focus on goals.

- Replace unhealthy coping mechanisms with healthier alternatives, such as taking a walk, meditating, or seeking support.

- Practice mindfulness to stay present and grateful in all aspects of life.

7. Find Accountability and Community

- Join a gym or fitness class that shares your values, like a faith-based fitness group.

- Participate in a life group or church community to foster accountability for both physical and spiritual growth.

- Identify a mentor or coach to guide you in maintaining a healthy composition.

8. Track Progress Holistically

- Journal physical, spiritual, and emotional growth weekly.

- Celebrate non-scale victories—like better sleep, improved energy, or deeper peace.

- Reflect on how a healthier body and spirit equips you to serve more fully.

Final Charge: Strength Through Balance

Your composition—physically, emotionally, and spiritually—reveals your stewardship. It reflects your priorities, your habits, and your heart. To live the Extraordinary Strength Life, you must align your outer body with your inner purpose. That means choosing strength, balance, and stewardship every day.

So ask yourself: Is your body helping you fulfill your mission—or holding you back from it?

Let's take care of the body God gave us. Let's strengthen our spiritual foundations. And let's walk forward in faith with full composure—mind, body, and spirit.

Because the extraordinary you is already within you. It's time to become one.

The Final Call: Strengthen the Vessel God Gave You

"Or do you not know that your body is a temple of the Holy Spirit within you, whom you have from God? You are not your own." — *1 Corinthians 6:19 (ESV)*

Your body is God's temple, and it's your responsibility to care for it. Caring for it is not optional—it's sacred. A strong body supports a strong mind and spirit. When you feel good, move well, and have energy, you show up fully in every role God has for you—spouse, parent, leader, servant, and follower of Christ.

Your body isn't just a machine to maintain—it's a temple to steward. It's the vessel God uses to carry out His mission through you. When your body is strong, healthy, and fueled with intention, it becomes a tool for service, impact, and worship.

In the Extraordinary Strength Method™, this holistic alignment of body, mind, and spirit is foundational. Each area fuels the other. When one grows stronger, the others follow. When one is neglected, the others suffer.

When even one cornerstone is neglected, your foundation is weakened. Let's revisit the truth from the introduction—and see how far you've come:

- Strong Mind but Weak Body = Vision Without Execution
- Strong Body but Weak Mind = Action Without Direction
- Strong Mind and Body but Weak Spirit = Burnout and Emptiness
- All Three Without Purpose = Strength Without Impact

Remember, these aren't just clever phrases—they are real consequences.

1. Strong Mind but Weak Body = Vision Without Execution

In Cornerstone 1, you built a mindset rooted in belief, discipline, responsibility, and perseverance. But if your body is too fatigued, inflamed, or unfit to act on that mindset—your vision will stall.

You'll know what to do, but won't have the strength to follow through.

You'll want to serve others, but lack the energy to show up.

You'll dream big—but your body will shut the door your mind wants to open.

That's why Cornerstone 2 matters so deeply: Because your body is the tool God uses to turn belief into action.

2. Strong Body but Weak Mind = Action Without Direction

On the other hand, physical strength without mental focus is wasted potential. It's movement without mission. Effort without alignment. Many people build their bodies but never renew their minds. They are disciplined in their workouts but undisciplined in thought. They chase fitness, but not purpose.

That's why these two cornerstones must go hand in hand. When your mindset is anchored in faith and your body is prepared by training, nutrition, and stewardship—you unlock a life that is not just strong, but significant.

Strength Through Stewardship

Your mind, body, and spirit are interconnected, and maintaining a healthy balance among them is essential for living the extraordinary life God has called you to. Taking care of your body is an act of worship and stewardship, ensuring that you have the energy, strength, and resilience to serve others and fulfill your purpose. You have greatness inside of you, but you must control your controllables. By prioritizing your health and spiritual life, you can overcome challenges and thrive in the life you were designed to live.

Maintaining a healthy body composition is not about achieving a societal standard but about living the extraordinary life God has called you to—free from preventable diseases and physical limitations. By striving for a healthy body fat percentage and stewarding your health wisely, you equip yourself to serve God and others more effectively. When you take control of your health now, you align yourself with God's desire for you to thrive and avoid the regret of inaction later. You can't control everything in life—but you can control what you eat, how you move, how you show up, and whether or not you invite God into your daily disciplines.

The Spiritual Parallel: Composed for Peace

A balanced spiritual life mirrors a healthy body composition. Just as excess body fat increases risks to physical health, an unbalanced spiritual life can lead to emotional, relational, and existential struggles.

Proverbs 4:23 (NIV) reminds us, *"Above all else, guard your heart, for everything you do flows from it."*

Engaging in regular spiritual practices like prayer, reading the Word, and serving others protects your heart and builds resilience, purpose, and peace. These habits shield you from stress, anxiety, and feelings of emptiness, strengthening your connection with God and with others.

Discipline Builds the Extraordinary

Whether in your training or your faith, discipline is the path. It's not always fun. It rarely feels easy. But it is always worth it. God's Word emphasizes the importance of discipline in all areas of life.

Hebrews 12:11(NIV) states, "*No discipline seems pleasant at the time, but painful. Later on, however, it produces a harvest of righteousness and peace for those who have been trained by it.*"

Discipline isn't punishment—it's preparation. It's planting seeds today for a harvest of strength, health, and peace tomorrow. Both your body and your spirit will reflect what you consistently pour into them. Just as physical health requires effort, intention, and consistency, so does spiritual growth. Both are disciplines that lead to abundant life when pursued faithfully.

Step Into the Extraordinary

God has placed greatness within you. Not just potential—but purpose. But it is your responsibility to steward your body, mind, and spirit well. Neglecting your health—physically or spiritually—can lead to consequences that hinder your ability to live out your calling. But when you take ownership of what you can control—your training, your nutrition, your mindset, and your faith—you become unstoppable.

Focus on what you can control. Fuel your body with nutritious foods, engage in regular strength and cardiovascular training, and prioritize spiritual growth.

Isaiah 40:31 (NIV) encourages us, *"But those who hope in the Lord will renew their strength. They will soar on wings like eagles; they will run and not grow weary, they will walk and not be faint."*

This Is Your Moment

You were created for more. You were designed to live a life that reflects the power, love, and strength of the God who made you. And when you bring your body, mind, and spirit into alignment, you step into that calling with confidence.

This isn't about perfection—it's about progress with purpose. Small, faithful steps in your training, nutrition, and spiritual walk will change your life. You don't have to have it all figured out. You just need to keep moving forward.

> *"I can do all this through Him who gives me strength."* — *Philippians 4:13 (NIV)*

Paul wrote these words not from a place of triumph, but from prison, teaching us that Christ's strength isn't just for achieving our goals, it's for finding contentment and peace in every circumstance, whether in abundance or need. This same strength that sustained Paul through hardship now empowers us to persevere in our calling, regardless of the obstacles we face.

So take the next step. Prioritize your health. Lean into your faith. Live with intention.

And become the extraordinary you God designed you to be.

Strengthen Your Body – Becoming the Vessel God Can Use

The Body Cornerstone is about more than fitness goals or appearance—it's about stewardship, strength, and purpose. Through the Extraordinary Strength Method™, you've been equipped with practical tools, spiritual truths, and habits to transform your physical health into a foundation for extraordinary living.

Let's recap the three pillars we've explored in this cornerstone:

Pillar 1: Training – Building Strength for Life and Purpose

Your body was created for movement, resilience, and power. Strength training and cardiovascular conditioning not only increase energy, mobility, and vitality—they build the grit and perseverance needed to live out your calling.

Through structured training using the Extraordinary Strength Method™, you learn to challenge self-limiting beliefs, develop mental toughness, and treat your workouts as a form of worship.

> *"Offer your bodies as a living sacrifice, holy and pleasing to God—this is your true and proper worship." — Romans 12:1 (NIV)*

Key Habit Highlights:

- Strength train 2–3 times per week

- Include cardiovascular training 1–3 times per week

- Practice consistency, progression, and intensity over time
- Use training as a tool to build mental resilience and spiritual endurance

Pillar 2: Nutrition – Fueling the Temple

You can't out-train a poor diet. Your nutrition is a daily act of stewardship and worship. What you eat either fuels your purpose or pulls you further from it.

This pillar taught you that food is fuel, and your diet is a reflection of your values. You learned to apply the 80/20 rule, practice mindful eating, and honor your body with clean, God-designed nutrition.

> *"Man shall not live by bread alone, but by every word that comes from the mouth of God."* — *Matthew 4:4 (ESV)*

Key Habit Highlights:

- Follow hand-based portion control for balanced meals
- Focus on whole, unprocessed foods ("from a plant, not made in a plant")
- Plan meals and stay consistent with your nutrition lifestyle— not short-term fads
- Give thanks for every meal and remain mindful of how and why you eat

Pillar 3: Body Composition – Reflecting Strength, Stewardship, and Purpose

This pillar moved beyond weight to focus on what truly matters—body composition and how it reflects your health and purpose. You learned how excess body fat increases risk for chronic disease, fatigue, and limited life potential—and how improving composition enhances every area of life.

> *"Beloved, I pray that all may go well with you and that you may be in good health, as it goes well with your soul."* — 3 John 1:2 (NIV)

By taking responsibility for your body composition through training, nutrition, and mindset, you honor God and position yourself to serve fully and live freely.

Key Habit Highlights:

- Measure progress through body fat percentage, not just weight
- Combine strength training, cardiovascular exercise, and clean eating to shift body composition
- Track your habits and stay accountable
- Focus on becoming capable, not perfect

Your body is not your own—it was given to you, and it's your responsibility to care for it. You can't outsource stewardship. You can't delegate discipline.

But you can take control of what you eat, how you move, and how you show up every single day.

When you strengthen your body, you sharpen your ability to carry out your calling.

When you care for your health, you care for your relationships, your energy, your service, and your worship.

Final Reflection:

You were created to be a vessel of strength, joy, and purpose. Your physical health is not just a personal priority—it's a spiritual responsibility.

When you align your training, nutrition, and body composition with God's Word and calling, you unlock your ability to live, lead, and love at your highest level. You don't need perfection—you need daily faithfulness.

"I can do all this through Him who gives me strength." — *Philippians 4:13 (NIV)*

- Are you treating your body like the temple God says it is?
- What would it look like to honor God with your health, training, and nutrition?
- How would strengthening your body help you fulfill your extraordinary purpose?
- Which habit can you commit to this week that brings your body into greater alignment with your faith?

Final Charge: Become the Vessel God Can Use

Are you ready to honor God with your body and step fully into His purpose for your life?

This isn't about chasing a six-pack or running marathons.

It's about being ready—physically, emotionally, and spiritually—to go where God calls and serve with everything you've got.

Take everything you've learned in this cornerstone and put it into action—not for vanity, but for victory. The habits, Scripture, and strategies in the Extraordinary Strength Method™ are your guide. Now it's your move.

Let your strength be your service. Let your discipline be your worship. Let your health be your offering.

What's Next: Awaken Your Spirit

You've renewed your mind.

You've strengthened your body.

But without a rooted spirit, even the sharpest mindset and strongest body will feel empty.

Here's the third danger to avoid:

Strong Mind and Body but Weak Spirit = Burnout and Emptiness

This is where many high achievers fall. They read all of the books. They hit the gym consistently. They crush their goals. But inside, they're hollow. Restless. Unfulfilled.

Because no matter how strong your mind and body become, if your spirit is weak—eventually, you'll burn out.

You'll run hard, but feel like you're going nowhere.

You'll check the boxes, but still feel disconnected.

You'll have energy and discipline, but lack joy and peace.

That's what happens when the source of strength is rooted in the self instead of in the Spirit of God.

When your faith is shallow, your motivation will dry up.

When your spirit is neglected, your strength becomes noise without meaning.

You weren't created just to perform—you were created to abide.

> *Jesus said, "I am the vine; you are the branches. If you remain in me and I in you, you will bear much fruit; apart from me you can do nothing." — John 15:5 (NIV)*

Without spiritual connection, physical and mental excellence eventually collapses under the weight of life. That's why the next cornerstone—Awaken Your Spirit—is essential. It doesn't just add meaning to your strength; it becomes the reason you keep going.

In the next section, you'll discover how to root your identity in Christ, fuel your purpose with faith, and build a spirit that can carry the weight of both mind and body so you can live fully, joyfully, and purposefully as the extraordinary you God created you to be

Let's go.

Awaken Your Spirit

You should now have a good understanding of how training your mind and body is paramount to a wonderful and successful life that is pleasing and honoring to God, that fulfills you and your purpose, and brings out that extraordinary you.

Hopefully you have been taking notes and implementing actions so far, and if so, I am proud of you! We have gone through a lot of information and actions that are important, but remember, not all of this can be changed all at once, but there should be positive action and change when learning anything.

Knowledge is only power with action, so make sure to take those small steps each day. Those small actions each day will lead you to the future that God is calling you to. This life route is not easy, but it is absolutely worth it. As we are entering our next cornerstone of the Extraordinary Strength Method together, we now focus on the part of us that cannot be trained with a barbell or a meal plan—our spirit.

Where My Spirit Awakened Into the Extraordinary

I have always enjoyed doing things for other people. It truly brings me joy. Even when I would learn something new that impacted me, I always wanted to share it with whoever I could so they could be impacted as well. This was such a massive part of why I fell in love with the Training for Warriors system.

The impact that it had on me just from a short seminar was insane. I knew that I wanted to share it with whoever I could so I could help them change their lives for the better. I knew this system was the way to do it. The values of this system are concrete, and the TFW Mission is to change and save lives. Sold. Let's do this!

The next step was finding a way to implement it at my current gym. God had much greater plans for me. During this time was when I was re-entering the church and really starting to rebuild my relationship with Jesus. At this point, I was seeing so many parallels between faith and fitness that it was like my pastor was talking directly to me every sermon. Through the inspiration and fire from Martin Rooney and the messages from God, I was ready to take that step and serve others at a higher level. This wasn't just about fitness anymore—this was about purpose.

Comparing what I was doing to what I could be doing, I knew that not only was I missing out on something huge, but so was everyone else. People would come into the gym, maybe socialize a little, workout a little, then go about their day and nothing would change. The biggest change happens not just in the body and mind, but when you are a part of something bigger than just yourself and you are following your purpose. This is spirit.

This is what the Extraordinary Strength Method™ is all about. True strength is not just physical or mental—it's spiritual. It's becoming the person God created you to be by strengthening all three. Spirit, I realized, is the deepest layer. It's where real transformation begins.

Spirit is defined as, "the nonphysical part of a person which is the seat of emotions and character of the soul." It is also defined as, "those qualities regarded as forming the definitive or typical elements in the character of a person." Your spirit is your emotions, your character, your heart. The decisions you make each day come down to this part of you.

If your character, your heart, your spirit is weak, the rest of you is weak. The reason I saved this portion for after Mind and Body is that this is the hardest one to work on and change. This part of you takes more time and effort. But, to lean into that extraordinary you, this is a must.

You can build habits, train hard, even master your mindset without a relationship with God—but awakening your spirit takes something more. It takes surrender. It takes divine strength.

Truly, all of the cornerstones and pillars beforehand can be changed without having a relationship with God, but for your spirit to change, this can only happen with God. Some say people cannot change, but I completely disagree. My life and who I am has been completely changed due to my relationship with Christ and giving my life to Him. I would not be who I am or where I am in life if it was not for Jesus.

My family raised me very well to be polite, honest, selfless, hardworking, and caring for others. But, I had a hard time controlling my emotions, specifically my anger, and after that season of depression and almost taking my own life, my anger was even harder to manage. That anger had to go somewhere, and working out was a fantastic outlet, but it really didn't fix my spirit. I was angry at God, and my heart and spirit needed work. I went a few years as a self-proclaimed atheist, saying I didn't believe in God. But again, how could I hate something that I was saying didn't exist? A part of me knew and believed in God, but I was broken. I just didn't want to face Him. Not yet.

Even though I was working out and taking better care of my body and mind, my spirit needed a lot of work. I was cynical. I did and said things without caring how it might affect someone else, and I was selfish. The way I was making myself think of it was that if I was going to get the short end of the stick by being the nice guy and trying to do more for others, then I would just focus on myself and do things for just me. That was honestly really hard for me. I felt a lot of guilt during this time, but I tried burying it deep down. I didn't want to be hurt again.

I still cared about my family and my friends, but I wasn't going to go out of my way for others or let myself get my heart destroyed again. I put up a massive wall around my heart and it hardened my spirit.

Along this journey through college, there was a massive spiritual battle going on inside of me. Part of me was trying to be the rough and tough guy that didn't have a care in the world. The guy that got all the girls but didn't get attached to anyone. The guy that didn't commit to anything seriously. The other part of me felt guilty when I treated people poorly and felt ashamed when I woke up the next day from drinking and couldn't remember what had happened the night before. The other part of me sought to make amends when I wronged someone and was desperate for something more. I was a walking contradiction. It was exhausting.

Everything shifted during my final semester when I started an internship at a gym in Erie. That's where I met two people who would change my life: Pastor Jack, and my now-wife, Lori Beth. She was working at the gym and immediately caught my attention. We didn't interact much at first, but once I got hired full-time, we worked side by side. Our friendship grew, but she made one thing clear: she wouldn't be with someone who didn't have a relationship with God. She told me she was attending a local church—and that Pastor Jack, a member at the gym, was actually the pastor there. That's when I started talking to him, too.

Between the two of them, the barriers I had put up started to come down. I was not ready to start going to church, but something was stirring.

Then, my world was rocked again—my mom was diagnosed with lung cancer. It felt like just as I was starting to put the pieces of my life together, everything fell apart. But God had positioned the right people in my life. Pastor Jack and Lori Beth were my anchors. Lori Beth shared how she had lost her brother and how her faith carried her through. That gave me the courage to go to church with her for the first time.

I realized then I was not going to be able to handle what was going on with my mom if I didn't get myself in the right spot, and I knew I couldn't do it on my own. I still wasn't set on the whole church and God thing, but it was worth a try.

The first few times were a bit awkward for me, but the messages were hitting me, a few of them bringing me to tears. I was able to handle the things going on with my mom better and didn't feel like I was completely falling apart. Then Lori Beth moved to Nashville for nursing school and I wasn't sure I would be able to go without her. But, something kept drawing me back in. My relationship with Lori Beth continued to grow stronger as my relationship with God grew stronger. I was becoming more confident in myself, I had more calmness with my mom's diagnosis, and my spirit was growing stronger.

I then decided to take that leap of faith after meeting Martin Rooney at that summit and go to the other gym to try to rebuild it with the Training for Warriors system. It was a huge risk but with the way things were going, I felt ready. But then another wrench was thrown in. Pastor Jack was leaving that church to go work with a national missions group. He was the only one I knew at that church so it wasn't the same without him there. I wasn't sure I could continue on this faith journey without having him around to talk with and keep me going.

Well, the weekends that Lori Beth was home, she had me try out different churches around us to see if we liked them. One of my friends invited us to Grace Church so we went with him one Sunday. That day was a true awakening for my spirit. I cried during worship and I cried during the sermon. It was like the floodgates of my spirit were opened.

Pastor Derek, their lead pastor, was speaking directly to me and into my life. The way his sermon aligned with what I was going through, with what I was learning through the Training for Warriors Affiliate course, it was like God was speaking to me directly.

Hebrews 4:12 (ESV) says it well. *"For the word of God is living and active, sharper than any two-edged sword, piercing to the division of soul and of spirit, of joints and of marrow, and discerning the thoughts and intentions of the heart."*

I couldn't shake the feeling. So I went back the following weekend and bam, the floodgates opened again and the sermon seemed to be God speaking to me directly again. This was crazy. I knew I had found where I was supposed to be. I can't tell you what was said those days, but I can tell you the feelings that I felt and how it directed me, I will never forget. The fire in me was undeniable. That's when I finally understood something Martin Rooney once said:

"We are all a part of something way bigger than just ourselves."

This was more than a system. This was more than a church. This was my divine awakening.

Your spirit is either of this world, or of God's Kingdom. What I mean by this is that your spirit is either directed by things of this world; money, power, position, accolades, etc. Or your spirit is directed by God's calling for your life. The purpose of your life will be directed by your spirit, your character.

If you do not have the Holy Spirit of God in you, then the purpose of your life is only of this world. This does not mean you will not do things selflessly, but when there is no bigger picture of life other than to live and to die, then most will choose to do things for themselves, since they only live once. But to truly be a part of something bigger than yourself and fulfill a much greater purpose, you have to have God with you, and when you have God with you, you will not fail!

Proverbs 19:21 (ESV), "*Many are the plans in the mind of a man, but it is the purpose of the LORD that will stand.*"

Throughout this cornerstone, we are going to break down the ways that it means to be a part of something bigger than yourself and how God will work in you and through you to fulfill your calling and your purpose to become the extraordinary you that God has made you to be.

> "*Each of you should use whatever gift you have received to serve others, as faithful stewards of God's grace in its various forms. If anyone speaks, they should do so as one who speaks the very words of God. If anyone serves, they should do so with the strength God provides, so that in all things God may be praised through Jesus Christ.*" – *1 Peter 4:10-11 (NIV)*

The Extraordinary Strength Method™ teaches us that purpose is not just something we pursue—it's something planted deep within us by God. Mind, body, and spirit must align to bring that purpose to life. For me, this was where all three finally came together. This was where I began stepping into the extraordinary.

And now, it's your turn.

Pillar 1: Serving Others

As part of the Extraordinary Strength Method™, service is how the spirit is trained, tested, and transformed. Just as the body must be strengthened through disciplined movement and the mind through renewed mindset, the spirit is refined through the practice of giving ourselves away—intentionally and sacrificially—for the good of others.

We have all been given gifts from God and are all made intricately and uniquely for His purpose in this life. Each one of us has something extraordinary to offer the world, and at the heart of that purpose is this truth: we were made to serve.

Imagine a world where people lived out their God-given gifts, not driven by selfish ambition, greed, and even envy of others but by desire to set out each day to do good for others. We would not live in the world we do today.

We are all a part of something bigger than ourselves, but many days get caught up in the rat race of life and all of the things of this world instead. Don't get me wrong, we are supposed to enjoy this world and all it has to offer, but not in the manner that puts people against other people and brings others down. Our gifts are given to us that we may bring joy to others and lift them up.

"The greatest thing you can do with all of your strength is to lift others up." - Martin Rooney

Proverbs 3:27 (ESV) says, *"Do not withhold good from those to whom it is due, when it is in your power to do it."*

You have something amazing to give the world and other people, it is not meant to be kept away in hiding, but to flourish and help others. Serving others has so many different avenues and faces—teaching, encouraging, mentoring, leading, listening—but no matter how it looks, real service flows from a heart aligned with God.

All forms of service have something in common; doing it because it is the right thing to do, and not expecting to be glorified for it. Don't do something kind for someone because you want to receive accolades and recognition for it. It is only true service when it is done without the expectation of something. We serve because it's what we were created to do. It's our spirit's workout.

This does not mean that you can't make serving others a career, though. It means that you are in that career for the service of others, not to get recognition for what you are doing. Serving others always gives back to the person serving, but it is not the reason we serve. It should be because it brings you joy to do so.

Like every other part of the Extraordinary Strength Method™, serving others requires training. Just as consistent effort in physical training builds strength and resilience, consistent acts of service build compassion, character, and purpose. Serving others isn't something we do once in a while—it's a lifestyle of intentional action that trains the spirit to be more like Christ.

> *"Not by the way of eye-service, as people-pleasers, but as bondservants of Christ, doing the will of God from the heart, rendering service with a good will as to the Lord and not to man, knowing that whatever good anyone does, this he will receive back from the Lord, whether he is a bondservant or is free." – Ephesians 6:6-8 (ESV)*

We live in a world that many expect to be served, that all things get handed to them, that they are entitled to it and are above others, but that is not what is intended for us. Scripture challenges us to live differently:

"Do nothing from selfish ambition or conceit, but in humility count others more significant than yourselves. Let each of you look not only to his own interests, but also to the interests of others." – Philippians 2:3-4.

This kind of service takes discipline. It's not easy to put others before yourself—especially when it costs you time, energy, or comfort. But discipline is one of the pillars of mental and spiritual strength, and like any muscle, it grows with training.

In the Extraordinary Strength Method™, we view mindful service like mindful movement: it's not just about doing the action, but being fully engaged in the process. Just as you wouldn't rush through a workout with poor form, don't rush through your service without intentional presence.

Be aware. Be invested. Be present. That's where transformation happens.

Example: Instead of quickly dropping off donations, spend time connecting with the people receiving them. Learn their names. Hear their stories. See their needs.

Just as perfect form engages the right muscles, mindful service engages the heart.

Just as physical fitness requires discipline and the sacrifice of comfort, spiritual fitness grows through acts of selflessness and serving others. Serving others mirrors the discipline needed in fitness and health—all involve setting aside personal desires and instant gratification for a greater good. To set aside ourselves to give in some way to someone else takes practice. Service can even be seen as the "workout" for the spirit.

Acts of kindness, compassion, and support toward others strengthen the spirit in the same way lifting weights strengthens the body.

Spiritual strength comes from repeated acts of giving and connecting with others. Like a fitness routine and a healthy lifestyle, serving others requires consistent effort and dedication. Spiritual health is maintained by regularly putting others' needs above your own, creating a disciplined lifestyle of compassion and empathy. Creating any disciplined type of lifestyle takes intentional thoughts and action. That means you have to seek ways to serve others, and when you seek it, you will find it. But it takes mindful intentionality to serve others.

Serving with intention parallels mindful movement in fitness. Just as you are conscious of your form and actions during a workout, mindful service—being fully present in the act of giving—enhances your spiritual connection and amplifies its impact on both the receiver and you. Serving with intention means you're not just doing something for the sake of fulfilling a duty or out of habit; you're fully present in that act of giving. You're considering the other person's needs, emotions, and situation, which creates a deeper impact.

Example: Instead of donating food to a shelter without much thought, you take time to learn what the shelter truly needs or even spend time with the recipients, building a personal connection.

Just as being conscious of your form in training ensures you're engaging the right muscles, being mindful in service ensures you're truly connecting with the person or the cause you're serving. You see them, listen to them, and understand their struggles or needs, which enhances the relational aspect of giving.

Example: Volunteering at a community center and engaging with the individuals there, rather than simply performing tasks, allows you to form bonds and share in their experiences.

Mindful service amplifies the spiritual connection between the giver and the receiver. When you serve with your heart fully engaged, the act becomes not only an external action but an internal spiritual exercise. You're reflecting on how the service contributes to both the other person's well-being and your own spiritual growth. When you serve others with intention, you amplify the effect of that service on both parties. Just as mindful movement in training produces better physical results and avoids injury, mindful service produces better emotional and spiritual outcomes, both for the giver and receiver.

For the receiver, the person receiving the service feels truly seen, valued, and heard, which can have a profound impact on their emotional and spiritual well-being. Acts of mindful service feel more personal, thoughtful, and meaningful.

For the giver, they experience a deeper sense of fulfillment and connection. Instead of serving as a transactional or routine act, the service becomes a transformative experience. The giver gains insight, personal growth, and a stronger sense of purpose, much like how mindful health practices benefit both the body and the mind.

> *"In all things I have shown you that by working hard in this way we must help the weak and remember the words of the Lord Jesus, how he himself said, 'It is more blessed to give than to receive.'" – Acts 20:35 (ESV)*

Both fitness and serving others transform us. Fitness transforms the body; service transforms the spirit. Each requires an investment of time, effort, energy, and intention but leads to greater personal and communal transformation. Each requires presence, focus, and a deep sense of purpose. When approached with intention, service can become a powerful tool for spiritual growth and becoming the extraordinary you God has called you to be.

This approach to service changes the game. It becomes more than a task—it becomes an act of worship. A spiritual discipline. A means through which God molds you and blesses others. When your heart is fully present in your service, it strengthens not only the one you serve but your own spirit too.

With taking care of your health, rest is essential for physical recovery. In spirituality, serving others can be exhausting if done without boundaries. This mirrors the need for balance between serving others and tending to your own spiritual health, avoiding burnout. There is a bit of selfishness that has to go with selflessness. You can't pour from an empty cup.

We are not able to take care of others if we cannot take care of ourselves, so if we are not healthy, we cannot serve others at the capacity that we should be able to. Our mind, body, and spirit needs to be tended to as well. That is why the above sections are so important. True wellness involves body, mind, and spirit.

Serving others allows the spirit to grow and our purpose to be fulfilled, but caring for oneself spiritually is also important. Acts of service should be paired with practices of prayer, meditation, and reflection, allowing for both giving and receiving.

This is why balance is essential in the Extraordinary Strength Method™. Your training, nutrition, rest, relationships, and service must work in harmony. If one falls too far out of alignment, the others suffer. Just as your muscles need recovery to grow, your spirit needs stillness, reflection, and time with God to stay strong and overflowing.

Your cup must also be filled. God's intention for you is that you are so filled that you overflow to all others around you, not for you to be empty. Taking time each day to care for your body, mind and spirit is needed.

Just as I talked about with your health, if you do not take time to take care of yourself, there will come a time when you have no choice and then you won't be able to take care of or serve others at all.

There will also be times in your life that you need others to care for you. You must allow others to serve you and overflow to you. When you deny blessings and service from others, that denies them the blessing of blessing you. It is okay to be served by others when it is something they want to do. They are filling their spirit and fulfilling their purpose as well.

Receiving is a part of the rhythm. Allow others to serve you. When you do, you honor their gifts and create a cycle of grace. It's not weakness to receive—it's humility, and it's a vital part of spiritual fitness.

But, we do not want to live life by others only serving us or expecting others to do so. No one is entitled to that kind of life, so it should never be an expectation. Serving others is the expectation and how you can truly fulfill your purpose and be the extraordinary you.

Ultimately, service is a reflection of your calling. It's the outward evidence of an inward transformation. It's where your purpose becomes visible. The more you serve, the more you discover who you were created to be. Find your gifts and give them to the world!

"Each of you should use whatever gift you have received to serve others, as faithful stewards of God's grace..." —1 Peter 4:10 (ESV)

Reflection Questions:

- What gifts has God given you, and how are you using them to serve others?

- Do you serve with a genuine heart, or do you sometimes seek recognition? How can you shift your mindset?

- How does serving others strengthen your spirit the way training strengthens your body?

- Are you balancing service and rest, or are you pouring from an empty cup?

- What's one area of service you can step into this week with full intention and presence?

- Are you willing to receive help? What might God be teaching you through that?

- How can you use your strength—physically, mentally, and spiritually—to lift others up today?

- Daily Mindful Intentions
  - Begin each day by setting an intention to serve at least one person—through kindness, prayer, or encouragement. Reflect at night on how it shaped your spirit.

- Purposeful Use of Gifts
  - Identify your God-given strengths and talents. Regularly find ways to apply them to uplift others at church, home, work, or in your community.

- Mindful Presence in Service
  - Be fully present. Listen deeply. Don't multitask your way through acts of kindness—slow down and connect.

- Balance Self-Care and Service
  - Just like in physical training, recovery matters. Schedule time for prayer, movement, and reflection. Protect your ability to serve long-term.

Bring It Together: Selfless Service in Action

- Discover Your Gifts
  - Journal or pray about your spiritual gifts. Ask people who know you well where they've seen you at your best.

- Find a Way to Serve Now
  - Choose a local ministry, neighbor, or a cause where you can apply your strengths. Commit to showing up at least once this month.

- Be Present in Your Service
  - During your next act of service, focus fully on the person or people in front of you. Listen. Connect. Be all in.

- Track & Reflect
  - Start a gratitude journal for your service. What did it cost you? What did it give you? What did God show you?

- Don't Pour from an Empty Cup
  - Dedicate time daily for Scripture, prayer, fitness, and reflection. Tend to your whole self so that your spirit can overflow with strength.

- Allow Others to Serve You:
  - Practice humility by graciously accepting help or gifts from others without guilt.

Final Charge: Make Service Your Superpower

Serving others is one of the most powerful ways to strengthen your spirit—it's an outward expression of the internal transformation God is doing in you. But service alone isn't the full picture. To truly walk in your purpose, the Extraordinary Strength Method™ reminds us that it's not just about action—it's about identity. It reminds us that service isn't a checklist—it's a calling. And your strength—mental, physical, and spiritual—was never meant to stop with you. It was meant to flow through you.

So serve boldly. Serve humbly. Serve consistently.

Let your service become the fruit of your transformation.

Let your actions reflect the One who gave everything to serve you.

Because when you live a life of selfless service, you don't just strengthen your spirit—you awaken your purpose.

The more you serve, the more God shapes your spirit. Your strength is not just measured in how much you give, but in the fruit your life produces as a result. This next pillar explores the spiritual traits that flow from a life fully aligned with God—what the Bible calls the Fruit of the Spirit. These are the markers of spiritual maturity and the evidence that you're becoming the extraordinary you God created you to be.

Pillar 2: Fruit of the Spirit

In the pursuit of becoming the extraordinary you, one truth must remain clear: your spirit is either aligned with the world or with God's Kingdom. As we learned earlier in the Extraordinary Strength Method™, true transformation doesn't just come from external behaviors or achievements—it begins in the heart, in the spirit. This is where lasting strength is built.

The Bible talks about things of this world being of the "flesh." In the Bible, the term "of the flesh" refers to a sinful tendency or power that leads people to seek their own will over God's.

Galatians 5:19–21 (ESV) gives us a sobering list: "*Now the works of the flesh are evident: sexual immorality, impurity, sensuality, idolatry, sorcery, enmity, strife, jealousy, fits of anger, rivalries, dissensions, divisions, envy, drunkenness, orgies, and things like these. I warn you, as I warned you before, that those who do such things will not inherit the kingdom of God.*"

These aren't just poor choices—they are signs of a life out of alignment with God's purpose.

But Galatians don't stop there. It shifts from the destructive to the divine: "*But the Fruit of the Spirit is love, joy, peace, patience, kindness, goodness, faithfulness, gentleness, self-control; against such things there is no law.*" – Galatians 5:22-23 (ESV)

Sounds like the world we live in is living in the flesh, doesn't it? Imagine if people lived by the Spirit, by the Fruit of the Spirit, and what kind of world we would be living in. It would be extraordinary. We may not be able to change the entire world, but we can sure make an impact on it. We do not have any control of how people act around us or what they do, but we have complete control of what we do and how we react to others. Living by the Fruit of the Spirit changes you and the world around you.

All of the things of the flesh are selfishness. These things put the single person's needs over the needs of everyone else. This is a character issue, a heart issue, a spirit issue. These things may seem fun at the moment, pretty much all sin is, otherwise it wouldn't be so tempting, but it always leads to either guilt, depression, or a continued longing to fill that void in your life and in your spirit.

Not one of us is perfect and can go throughout life without some of this happening, but if you want to inherit the kingdom of God and fulfill your purpose, a spirit-led life is how to do it. The Fruit of the Spirit is not just things to think on and value, it is a call to action, because a value is not what we think about all the time, it is what we do all of the time. To strengthen your spirit, acting on the Fruits of the Spirit is how to do it. All of these are intertwined and are an integral part of living out an extraordinary life.

These nine fruits are not simply traits to admire. They are the internal evidence of a life filled with the Spirit—lived with intentionality, rooted in faith, and aligned with purpose. And just like in physical training, they require effort, repetition, and refinement.

In the Extraordinary Strength Method™, we teach that mental and physical discipline must be matched with spiritual alignment to achieve true wholeness. The Fruit of the Spirit represents the spiritual reps we put in each day—not for applause or recognition, but for alignment with the character of Christ.

Each fruit is a spiritual muscle. Some may already be stronger than others in your life. Others may feel weak or underdeveloped. That's okay—just like with physical training, strength is built through small, consistent, intentional reps.

This isn't about being perfect—it's about being faithful in your pursuit of extraordinary strength. A spirit led by God, shaped by His Word, and trained in the Fruit of the Spirit will not only change your life—it will overflow into the lives of others.

Love—The Foundation of Strength

1 Corinthians 13:4–8a (ESV) says, *"Love is patient and kind; love does not envy or boast; it is not arrogant or rude. It does not insist on its own way; it is not irritable or resentful; it does not rejoice at wrongdoing, but rejoices with the truth. Love bears all things, believes all things, hopes all things, endures all things. Love never ends."*

Love is the starting point. It's the first fruit for a reason. Everything else—joy, peace, patience, even discipline—flows from a heart that is grounded in love.

But love, the way Scripture defines it, is not soft or passive. It is action. It is a sacrifice. It is strength under control. Love is the spiritual core of the Extraordinary Strength Method™—it activates purpose, fuels perseverance, and gives meaning to every rep, every choice, every moment of service.

This action is to love yourself and to love others. Yes, you must love yourself. This is not narcissistic love where you put yourself above all others, it is the love of yourself that you take care of your mind, body, and spirit so you may live out your purpose and serve and love others.

Loving others is not just those that you get along with, have the same in common with, or are related to, it is loving those that you disagree with, are rivals with, and even those that are your enemy. Many talk about loving others while at the same time giving hate to those that are different from them in their personal, political, and religious beliefs.

Political parties are the worst at this right now. Claiming that they love others while creating divide and hate for all those that do not side with them. But to truly love others is loving all others, even if you don't agree with them, their lifestyle, their actions, or their beliefs. You do not have to condone what they are doing, but you can still show them love. Sharing truth with others is a great form of love, but it has to be done with kindness and grace.

It is not a "holier than thou" type of truth either, it is caring for the person and wanting the absolute best for them and sharing with them truth that can help them, but again, it must be done with kindness and grace.

In the Extraordinary Strength Method™, we train our bodies with discomfort to grow physically. Likewise, we must train our hearts to love when it's uncomfortable to grow spiritually. Every act of love—especially when it's difficult—is a spiritual rep that strengthens your character and aligns you with Christ.

This kind of love doesn't look for applause or reciprocation. It is love because it is rooted in truth. And it expresses that truth with kindness and grace.

If you want to strengthen your spirit and step into the extraordinary life God has for you, this is the first step: Love well. Love intentionally. Love like Jesus.

Joy—Fuel for the Journey

John 15:11 (ESV) says, "*These things I have spoken to you, that my joy may be in you, and that your joy may be full.*"

Joy is defined as "a feeling of great pleasure and happiness."

Joy is deeper than happiness. It's not based on how your day is going, how much money is in your account, or whether you feel like everything's going your way. Joy is internal strength rooted in something unshakable—your relationship with God.

In the Extraordinary Strength Method™, we talk about sustainable progress. That doesn't happen without consistent fuel. Spiritually, joy is that fuel. It's what keeps you going when the workout gets hard, when the mission feels unclear, or when life doesn't make sense.

In the Bible, joy is a lasting emotion that comes from trusting in God's promises, an internal state of being, rooted in a person's communion with Christ and peace of spirit. True joy is a response to what God delights in, and requires you to have values that align with God's. Joy is long-lasting and can be present even in the face of trials and tribulations.

Joy is a Fruit of the Spirit because it doesn't come naturally. It's produced through walking closely with God—trusting His promises, even when your circumstances seem to contradict them. It's a decision to believe that even in the mess, God is still working. It's strength that smiles in the storm—not because of the storm, but because of who walks with you through it.

Joy doesn't deny reality, but it defies despair. It doesn't pretend that pain doesn't exist—it just knows that pain doesn't get the final word.

In your training, there are moments when the weight feels heavy. In your faith, there will be seasons when the burden is emotional, mental, or spiritual. That's when joy kicks in. It reminds you of your why. It lifts your chin. It resets your focus from frustration to faith.

Joy is also contagious. When you walk in joy, you shift atmospheres. You become the light in someone else's dark day. You give hope just by being steady. And let's be honest—there is a strength in joy that no barbell can touch. It's the supernatural energy that allows you to keep showing up with purpose, even when everything around you tells you to quit.

Joy, like the other fruits, grows through practice. And when it's rooted in your purpose and powered by your faith, it becomes a non-negotiable piece of your extraordinary strength.

Peace—Strength in Stillness

Philippians 4:7 (ESV) says, *"And the peace of God, which surpasses all understanding, will guard your hearts and your minds in Christ Jesus."*

Peace is more than the absence of chaos—it's the presence of God in the middle of it.

In the Extraordinary Strength Method™, peace is your foundation. Just like you need a stable base to lift heavy weight, you need a spiritually grounded base to carry the weight of life. Without peace, everything wobbles. But when peace is present—deep, unshakable, Spirit-filled peace—you can stand firm no matter what's shaking around you.

Peace is defined as "freedom from disturbance; tranquility." The Hebrew word for *peace* is shalom, which means "completeness," "soundness," and "well-being." Shalom is the result of right relationships with God, others, and creation. Peace is what happens when your thoughts, your actions, and your spirit are aligned with God's will.

The Bible describes peace as a work of the Holy Spirit, a state of inner repose and quietness that can be experienced even in adverse circumstances. To have true peace, you need:

1) Spiritual Peace, which is peace with God

2) Relational Peace, which is peace with others, and

3) Emotional Peace, which is peace within ourselves.

Peace involves a deep acceptance of oneself, including both strengths and weaknesses, and a willingness to embrace life with an open heart and mind. When your will and actions are aligned with God's will and calling for you, when you love and live peaceably with others, and when you love and are peaceable with yourself, you will experience true peace, no matter what trials or circumstances may be going on in your life.

We live in a world filled with noise—constant alerts, opinions, anxiety, pressure. That's why peace is such a powerful fruit. It's not passive. It's active. It guards your heart and your mind like a trained warrior. It shields you from panic. It silences the lie that tells, "You're not enough," or "This will never get better."

This kind of peace only comes through the Holy Spirit. And just like a healthy body needs rest and recovery, your spirit needs space to breathe and reconnect with its source. When you create intentional rhythms of rest—through prayer, Scripture, worship, reflection—you make room for peace to grow.

Peace doesn't mean you stop moving forward. It means you move forward without fear. You train. You lead. You fight. But you do it with a calm assurance that God's got it under control—even when you don't.

Extraordinary strength doesn't come from force alone. Sometimes it comes from stillness. From surrender. From the quiet confidence that, no matter what, God is with you, for you, and working through you.

Patience—Strength Through Endurance

> *Colossians 3:12-14 (ESV), "Put on then, as God's chosen ones, holy and beloved, compassionate hearts, kindness, humility, meekness, and patience, bearing with one another and, if one has a complaint against another, forgiving each other; as the Lord has forgiven you, so you also must forgive. And above all these put on love, which binds everything together in perfect harmony."*

Patience is the ability to wait well. It's spiritual endurance in action.

In the Extraordinary Strength Method™, we often talk about embracing the process. Whether it's building physical strength, changing body composition, or mastering a new habit—results take time. You don't get stronger from one workout. You don't build endurance from one run. And you certainly don't transform your spirit overnight.

Patience is the fruit that trains your spirit to stay the course.

Patience is defined as "the capacity to accept or tolerate delay, trouble, or suffering without getting angry or upset."

In the Bible, patience is the ability to endure trials, wait for a promise to be fulfilled, or persevere toward a goal. It's also the capacity to tolerate delays or challenges without becoming frustrated, angry, or upset.

It's not just about tolerating delay—it's about growing during delay. It's choosing faith over frustration. It's showing grace in the waiting, when you're tempted to give up or take control. It's what allows you to keep moving forward, even when you're not seeing the results yet.

This is spiritual strength forged in the fire of frustration. Anyone can keep going when things are easy. But the extraordinary you is built in the trials, when your timeline doesn't match God's, and you choose to trust Him anyway.

Patience is a value that can be developed and strengthened through God's power and goodness. It's also a spiritual discipline that can lead to greater faith, hope, wisdom, resilience, and calm. This is paired with what we talked about earlier in the book: perseverance. There are many biblical references to patience and perseverance, and fulfilling your purpose will take great patience and perseverance.

Just like progressive overload in training, patience increases your capacity over time. It stretches your spirit so that what once made you snap now makes you pray. What once made you quit now makes you push. You develop spiritual stamina.

And here's what's amazing: Patience isn't weakness. It is power under control. It's the kind of power that lets you hold back when your flesh says "rush." It's the strength to wait with peace, move with purpose, and act in alignment with God's timing.

Patience isn't passive. It's training. It's resistance. It's growth.

Kindness—Strength Through Compassionate Action

"Thus says the Lord of hosts, Render true
judgments, show kindness and mercy to one
another." – Zechariah 7:9 (ESV)

Kindness is defined as "the quality of being friendly, generous, and considerate."

Kindness is one of the most misunderstood forms of strength. Our culture often views kindness as weakness—but in the Kingdom of God and through the lens of the Extraordinary Strength Method™, kindness is a form of power. It is strength under control, directed outward to serve others with compassion and grace.

In the Bible, kindness is defined as a selfless, compassionate, and merciful act that is rooted in love. It is more than just being tolerant or nice to people, but rather involves showing goodness, generosity, and sympathy toward others. The Hebrew word for kindness is *hesed*, which means "loving-kindness." It describes the way God loves his people, and also the love and mercy of God toward humanity.

True kindness isn't just "being nice." It's intentional. It's rooted in action. Just like training your body takes focused reps and effort, training your spirit through kindness requires consistency, awareness, and follow-through.

This Fruit of the Spirit is deeply connected to the Serving Others pillar. It's how strength gets transferred—not through domination, but through gentleness and care. Whether it's encouraging someone during a hard season, offering forgiveness when it's undeserved, or simply listening without judgment, kindness is a spiritual muscle in motion.

And like muscle, kindness can be strengthened.

Every day offers small but powerful opportunities to train it. It could be showing grace in traffic instead of reacting with anger. Holding your tongue when criticism rises up. Checking in on someone you haven't seen in a while. Smiling at the cashier. These aren't just "nice things"—they're reps of righteousness. They build the kind of spirit that lifts others up.

In the gym, we know that you grow where you're weakest—if you're willing to work that area. The same goes for kindness. If it's hard for you to extend grace, be intentional about doing it. If you struggle to forgive, start practicing it. Just like fitness, the more you train it, the stronger and more natural it becomes.

Kindness is one of the most visible signs of spiritual maturity—and when you live with it consistently, you don't just change others—you change you.

Acting on kindness looks something like this:

- Be kind to everyone, especially those that are different from you.

- Love your enemies: Jesus said to love your enemies, do good, and give while expecting nothing in return.

- Put others above yourself.

- Forgive one another.

- Be kind with your words and deeds: Kindness involves using the right words and gestures, and showing consideration for all people.

Just as the other Fruits of the Spirit, kindness is rooted in love.

Like wildfire, kindness will spread and change all those around it. In all situations, use kindness, for as Robin Williams said, "*Remember, everyone you meet is fighting a battle you know nothing about. Be kind. Always.*" For a fulfilled and extraordinary life, kindness will never do you wrong.

Goodness—Holiness in Action That Lifts Others

> *"Every good gift and every perfect gift is from above, coming down from the Father of lights, with whom there is no variation or shadow due to change." – James 1:17 (ESV)*

Goodness is defined as "the quality of being morally good or virtuous." Goodness isn't just about "being a good person." It's doing what's right—even when it's inconvenient, uncomfortable, or unseen. Goodness is holiness in action, and it's one of the clearest outward expressions of an extraordinary spirit. It is a quality that comes from God and is intended to benefit others.

Through the Extraordinary Strength Method™, we understand that every cornerstone of transformation—mental, physical, spiritual, and purposeful—requires consistent action. Goodness is no exception. It's not passive. It's not about appearing virtuous. It's about taking deliberate steps toward righteousness, even when no one's watching.

Goodness is what fuels integrity. It's what keeps you doing the right thing even when it costs you time, energy, or recognition. It's holding yourself to a higher standard—not out of pride, but because you know that your actions carry weight. That they matter. That they influence and inspire.

It's saying the hard truth in love. It's choosing to help someone when it would be easier to walk away. It's keeping a promise when it would be simpler to quit.

Goodness, in essence, is the bridge between your values and your actions. It's how belief becomes behavior. And this is where the transformation truly happens.

You don't train for strength just to look strong—you train so you're prepared to lift something (or someone) when the time comes. In the same way, you cultivate goodness so when life gives you the opportunity to stand up, speak out, or serve well, you're ready.

Goodness is contagious. It elevates everyone around you. It brings light into dark places. And most importantly, it aligns you with the example of Christ—the One who embodied perfect goodness for the sake of others. He died on the cross to give people the gift of eternal life, and His ministry is described as doing good and healing others.

Read this again, goodness is holiness in action intended to benefit others. Goodness encapsulates kindness in action and doing the right thing. It is not always easy to do good or do the right thing, but it will always strengthen your spirit and lead to more extraordinary things in your life.

Faithfulness—The Discipline of Steadfast Commitment

"Steadfast love and faithfulness meet; righteousness
and peace kiss each other." – Psalm 85:10 (ESV)

"Now faith is the assurance of things hoped for, the
conviction of things not seen. By faith we understand
that the universe was created by the word of God,
so that what is seen was not made out of things
that are visible." – Hebrews 11:1–3 (ESV)

Faithfulness is more than belief—it's commitment in action. It's the discipline of showing up consistently, even when your emotions don't feel like it, when results aren't instant, or when it's hard.

In the Extraordinary Strength Method™, discipline is a pillar of mental strength, and faithfulness is where that discipline meets devotion. It's one thing to feel inspired for a moment. It's another to walk in that inspiration daily, regardless of outcomes.

Faithfulness is what carries your purpose from idea to impact.

The term faithful is defined as "remaining loyal and steadfast." In the Bible, faithfulness is defined as a virtue that involves unwavering commitment, loyalty, reliability, and trustworthiness to God and to others. Faithfulness is also about keeping promises, honoring covenants, and following through on commitments. This is a main attribute of God. He is always faithful, past, present, and future, and always delivers on His promises.

We fall extremely short of this as humans and is something to be continuously worked on. In your relationship with God, it's staying in the Word, staying in prayer, and trusting Him—especially when you don't understand. In your relationships with others, it's honoring your commitments, keeping your word, and showing up with consistency.

Just like you don't build physical strength overnight, faithfulness is forged through repetition. Through daily spiritual training. Through obedience in the unseen. Through showing up to serve, love, and lead even when it costs you.

Faithfulness also speaks to your trust in God's timing and promises. In seasons of waiting, in the face of uncertainty, faithfulness declares, "God, I trust You anyway."

It's one of the most powerful forms of strength you can develop— because it's not just about you. Your faithfulness strengthens those around you. It builds credibility, encourages others to persevere, and reflects the unwavering faithfulness of God Himself.

> *"He who calls you is faithful; He will surely do it." — 1 Thessalonians 5:24 (ESV)*

Being extraordinary doesn't require being flashy. It requires being faithful. And in a world full of inconsistency and distraction, your faithfulness will set you apart.

Gentleness—Strength Under Control

> *"Let your gentleness be evident to all. The Lord is near."— Philippians 4:5 (NIV)*

Gentleness is often misunderstood. In today's culture, it's sometimes seen as weakness or passivity. But in the Kingdom of God—and through the lens of the Extraordinary Strength Method™—gentleness is actually one of the greatest expressions of true strength.

Gentleness is "the quality of being kind, tender, or mild-mannered."

In the Bible, gentleness is defined as the quality of being kind, tender, and mild-mannered, or the ability to correct someone without harshness. It is strength under control. It's power with purpose. It's the ability to respond rather than react.

In training, we learn that brute force isn't enough—you need technique, timing, and the ability to control your strength. The same is true in your spirit. Gentleness is a spiritual technique. It's knowing when to speak and when to listen. When to challenge and when to comfort. When to stand firm and when to soften.

Jesus modeled gentleness masterfully. He had the power to calm storms, raise the dead, and command legions of angels—but He also knelt to wash feet, welcomed children, and lifted the broken and rejected. His spirit was both mighty and meek. That is the kind of extraordinary spirit we're after.

Gentleness is also a discipline—a spiritual habit that must be trained and reinforced. It requires humility, patience, and emotional strength to pause before responding. But just like in fitness, that pause is where your power grows.

> *"A gentle answer turns away wrath, but a harsh word stirs up anger." — Proverbs 15:1 (NIV)*

In the Extraordinary Strength Method™, gentleness aligns with the mental and spiritual strength pillars of self-mastery, humility, and emotional control. It's about mastering your inner world so that your external actions reflect the character of Christ.

When you respond to others with gentleness, especially in moments where the world would expect anger, sarcasm, or retaliation—you become a mirror of grace. You create peace in conflict, soften hardened hearts, and reflect the Spirit of God through your restraint.

Gentleness doesn't weaken your impact—it multiplies it.

Self-Control—Master the Inner War

2 Timothy 1:7 (ESV) says, *"for God gave us a spirit not of fear but of power and love and self-control."*

Self-control might be the final Fruit of the Spirit listed in Galatians, but don't mistake it for the least. In fact, without self-control, the other fruits lose their foundation. Without self-control, love turns reactive, joy becomes circumstantial, and peace quickly fractures.

This is the fruit that holds the others together—and it's the cornerstone of your spiritual strength.

In the Extraordinary Strength Method™, self-control is the ultimate expression of discipline. It's where the mind, body, and spirit intersect. It's what allows you to say "no" to temptation, "yes" to purpose, and "not yet" when the world shouts "right now."

The definition of self-control is "the ability to control oneself, in particular one's emotions and desires or the expression of them in one's behavior, especially in difficult situations."

In the Bible, self-control is a virtue that involves controlling one's thoughts, words, actions, and desires, especially in challenging situations.

Just like physical training builds strength through consistent resistance, self-control is forged through daily choices in the face of spiritual, emotional, and cultural resistance.

We live in a world of endless instant gratification—dopamine-driven scrolling, impulse spending, emotional outbursts, and food addictions masked as "self-care." But true self-control—extraordinary self-control—looks beyond the moment and sees the mission.

> *"A man without self-control is like a city broken into*
> *and left without walls." — Proverbs 25:28 (ESV)*

Without spiritual boundaries, the enemy has easy access. Without discipline, purpose erodes. But when you commit to training your spirit with the same focus you train your body—through prayer, Scripture, accountability, and aligned daily habits—you begin to build walls of strength that the enemy cannot scale.

This isn't about willpower alone. Self-control is a Fruit of the Spirit, not the flesh. That means your strength comes from God. The more you abide in Him, the more control you gain over the parts of yourself that once felt out of control.

In the Extraordinary Strength Method™, this is the "grind" that most people overlook—the small, daily, quiet victories no one sees. The morning you chose prayer over the snooze button. The meal you skipped to fast and seek God. The argument you diffused by holding your tongue. The workout you showed up to when everything in you wanted comfort instead.

These small wins compound into spiritual momentum. And that momentum transforms you into someone who doesn't just try to live by the Spirit—but is led by the Spirit.

Self-control is the final link in the chain, and when you train it intentionally, the extraordinary life God has called you to isn't just possible but becomes inevitable—it creates an unbreakable spirit and an extraordinary life. There is no greater purpose and fulfillment in life that happens without self-control. For you to become the extraordinary you, a spirit of self-control must be built. Deny that temptation, fight against the urges of the flesh and of this world to become the extraordinary you!

Becoming the Extraordinary You—One Fruit at a Time

The journey isn't about perfection, but faithful progress.

As you've seen, the Fruit of the Spirit isn't just a checklist of character traits—it's a daily training ground for spiritual growth. Just like physical strength is developed through progressive resistance, spiritual strength is developed by choosing love over anger, patience over frustration, joy over negativity, and self-control over instant gratification—repeatedly.

Each fruit works in tandem with the others, building a resilient, Christ-centered character. This is what it means to awaken your spirit and train it through the Extraordinary Strength Method™— where discipline, discomfort, and devotion collide to produce lasting transformation.

You won't embody these fruits perfectly, and that's okay. But through intentional action and dependence on God's power, you can grow stronger each day. Every slip is an opportunity to grow. Every act of love, joy, peace, patience, kindness, goodness, faithfulness, gentleness, or self-control is a rep that strengthens your spirit for your God-given purpose.

The more you practice these fruits, the more your life will reflect God's presence. The extraordinary life isn't about achieving perfection—it's about becoming who God has called you to be through daily spiritual training.

So reflect, realign, and recommit to the process. One fruit at a time, one action at a time, you are becoming the extraordinary you.

Reflection Questions

- Which Fruit of the Spirit do you feel God has already begun to grow in you?

- Which Fruit do you struggle with most—and what one action can you take today to strengthen it?

- How do you typically react in moments of stress, temptation, or offense? What would it look like to respond in the Spirit instead?

- How would your relationships change if you lived out just one of these fruits more consistently?

- Who in your life reflects the Fruit of the Spirit well—and what can you learn from them?

- In what area of your life are you most in need of spiritual discipline right now?

Habits to Build: Cultivating the Fruit of the Spirit

Like physical strength, spiritual fruit grows through consistent training. These habits are the spiritual "reps" that will shape your character and transform your life:

- Love – Practice selfless love daily, even toward those who challenge you.

- Joy – Choose joy as a mindset rooted in faith, not dependent on circumstance.

- Peace – Create space for inner stillness by aligning with God's will.

- Patience – Respond with grace and calm rather than emotion or impulse.

- Kindness – Be known for intentional kindness in your tone, words, and actions.

- Goodness – Act with integrity even when no one is watching.

- Faithfulness – Stay rooted in God's promises and loyal in your relationships.

- Gentleness – Lead with humility, even when you've been wronged.

- Self-Control – Discipline your impulses by surrendering them to God daily.

Bringing It Together: Spiritual Strength in Action

Let these small but powerful actions shape how you live each day:

- Love – Write down one way you'll care for your mind, body, and spirit today—then one way you'll show love to someone difficult.

- Joy – Start a gratitude journal. Write down three small joys or signs of God's goodness daily.

- Peace – Spend five minutes in silence and prayer each day. Breathe. Release anxiety.

- Patience – Identify a situation that tests you. When it arises, pause. Pray. Respond with peace.

- Kindness – Perform one intentional act of kindness today and reflect on how it felt.

- Goodness – Choose integrity over convenience in one specific situation this week.

- Faithfulness – Meditate on a promise from Scripture. Show up for your calling and others—even when it's hard.

- Gentleness – Identify a past or present offense. Pray over it. Forgive or offer grace.

- Self-Control – Identify one area where you feel undisciplined—your habits, words, or thoughts. Set one new boundary and hold it for one week.

Final Charge: Live Strong in Spirit

Stay steadfast. Remember, spiritual transformation is like any training—it's not about perfection, but progress. One rep at a time. One choice at a time.

Spiritual fruit doesn't grow by accident. It grows through intention, action, and daily surrender. Each fruit represents the strength of your Spirit at work—shaped not by perfection, but by persistence.

This is what the Extraordinary Strength Method™ is all about—becoming more like Christ from the inside out.

You are building spiritual strength. You are living the Extraordinary Strength Method™ from the inside out. And this isn't just for you. This fruit is meant to feed others too, it's meant to nourish others, reflect the heart of God, and fuel your extraordinary life.

So keep showing up. Keep growing. Keep choosing the next faithful action.

You've got work to do—and you're not doing it alone.

You're being called to live out an extraordinary life.

One choice at a time. One fruit at a time. One day at a time.

When we allow the Fruit of the Spirit to guide our character, our inner life begins to reflect God's nature—love, peace, patience, joy, and so much more. But even with a spirit aligned with God, we are not meant to carry this journey alone. The extraordinary life we are called to live isn't a solo mission—it's a shared one.

To become who God has truly called you to be, you must walk with others, support others, and allow others to support you. Because we are not meant to go through this life alone.

Let's go.

Pillar 3: Strength in Unity—We Are Not Meant To Go Through Life Alone

We Are Stronger Together

"If you want to go fast, go alone. If you want to go far, go together." - African Proverb

Being a part of something bigger than yourself is truly rewarding, but very difficult at times. It is hard to find the balance between serving others to the best of your ability and serving too much. By this I mean that you do not want to be so focused on serving others that you do not allow others to serve you, especially when you need it most. This is having a humble spirit.

I, for one, used to be very stubborn in letting other people help me, but a great friend of mine once told me, "if you deny me to bless you, you are denying the ability for me to get blessed as well."

When we serve and help others, we are always going to be blessed and served in return. It is okay to receive help. You have to be humble enough in spirit to know that you cannot handle everything on your own. We are not meant to go through life alone or without any help from others.

That's the beauty of community—blessing goes both ways. We are not built for isolation. We are not designed to carry the weight of life alone. God designed us for unity, and unity is a powerful component of the Extraordinary Strength Method™. Your strength doesn't come only from what you can do on your own—it comes from your ability to stand shoulder to shoulder with others, share the load, and grow together.

Ecclesiastes 4:9-12 (ESV) says, "*Two are better than one, because they have a good reward for their toil. For if they fall, one will lift up his fellow. But woe to him who is alone when he falls and has not another to lift him up! Again, if two lie together, they keep warm, but how can one keep warm alone? And though a man might prevail against one who is alone, two will withstand him—a threefold cord is not quickly broken.*"

Unity in Purpose: Each Part Matters

We are made stronger through Christ and through the people He places in our lives. That's part of your spiritual design—to strengthen others where they are weak and be strengthened where you fall short. This is the heart of what it means to be extraordinary: using your God-given strengths not just for your benefit, but for the benefit of others.

This is why God made Eve for Adam because he did not want him to be alone and knew he would need her. He knew Adam needed help, connection, and companionship. We all do.

You weren't created to be self-sufficient in every area. You were created for connection, contribution, and collaboration. Whether it's a spouse, mentor, coach, friend, teammate, or church family, you need others—and they need you.

This is why unity is one of the foundational traits of the Extraordinary Strength Method™. True strength is never about standing alone. It's about linking arms with others, working toward a shared mission, and understanding that you are a vital piece of something greater.

Unbreakable: The Power of a Unified Spirit

This truth has stood the test of time. One of the oldest illustrations of unity comes from Aesop's fable:

"A Father had a family of sons who constantly fought with one another. One day, he gathered them together and handed each a bundle of sticks. He asked them to break the bundle. One by one, they failed. Then he untied the bundle and gave them each a single stick. They snapped easily.

'Do you not see,' the Father said, 'that if you stand united, you are unbreakable—but divided, you are fragile?'"

That story carries the same message as one of the most quoted Scriptures on unity:

> "As iron sharpens iron, so one person sharpens another." – Proverbs 27:17 (NIV)

You will need the strength of others in your life, just as they will need yours.

This is the backbone of spiritual strength in the Extraordinary Strength Method™: you grow in purpose and power when you grow together. No one fulfills their calling in isolation. You may be able to go fast alone, but you'll only go far when you go together.

Carrying the Yoke Together

Many challenges in life are made to be conquered with others, and having others there to help sharpen you and give you the strength needed to overcome them. When these types of challenges arrive, you have to put away your ego and pride or it could likely destroy you. Be willing to accept help and be lifted by others because "a rising tide lifts all ships."

By allowing others to help you and you help them, we all get better together. No idea, invention, or anything made by humans happened without some sort of help from others. You show true strength when you allow others to step in and help you.

Yes, people will fail you and disappoint you, but nobody is perfect. Everyone makes mistakes and drops the ball. This is no reason to be a loner in life. It is a miserable life to be alone without anyone there to share life with, let alone to have others there to help you when you need it.

> *"A friend loves at all times, and a brother is born*
> *for a time of adversity." – Proverbs 17:17 (NIV)*

Others are to be there for times of adversity, not just the good times. The relationships that are built through conquering challenges together are often unbreakable. There is a bond created unlike anything else.

Now, this does not mean that you should not give your best effort in overcoming things and rely on others to do it for you. Not at all. There is always work to be done by all. When others step in to help, they are not coming in to take the entire load off your back, but to share the yoke. This means you have to carry your own weight, just as they are carrying theirs.

I believe some mistake the idea of not going through life alone to mean that others should always be helping them and doing things for them. You have to earn help from others by working through it with them helping alongside you, and then also stepping in to help them when they are in need.

If you take advantage of people's help, they will be less likely to step in to aid you when you are in need again. Don't be the one leaning on a shovel praying for a hole or telling others how to dig it as you stand there, step in and do the work together. If you are willing to take action in conquering your fears and challenges, others will be there to help you.

When you're humble enough to be helped and strong enough to help others—you become unstoppable. That's the extraordinary spirit God designed in you.

Face the Lion—Together

Here is a great story we tell in TFW that describes this well:

A young buffalo once asked his Dad, "Hey Dad, what's the scariest thing in the world?"

The father buffalo told him it was a lion! Because lions eat buffalo.

The young buffalo thought to himself for a moment and then said, "OK Dad, if I ever see a lion, I'll run away in the other direction as fast as I can!"

But the Dad said that's actually the opposite of what he should do. He then gave his son this wise advice. "Son, when you see a scary lion, you should stand your ground. Look the lion straight in the eye. Stomp your feet. Show off your sharp horns. Maybe even try charging at the lion as fast as you can!"

And the son responded, "But Dad, I am so small and he is so big, how could I take him on?"

The father smiled and said, "Look around at the other 200 buffalo here, son. If you run away, the lion will probably catch you and eat you. But if you stay with our pack, if you charge that lion, you have 200 other buffalo friends with sharp horns who will fight with you. We help each other when facing scary lions. If you run away, we can't help you."

The buffalo knows the power of being a part of something bigger, having others in your corner, and also the dangers of running away from your fears and obstacles.

Something that also makes a big difference is who you have in your corner with you, the people you surround yourself with. They are either going to be the biggest help or the biggest hindrance of you growing and overcoming the challenges of life.

Family, Faith, and Who You Surround Yourself With

As we talked about previously, your friend circles will change and ideally get better as you grow, but one thing you cannot change is those you are related to; your family.

Family is defined as "a group of people related to one another by blood or marriage." Now we all know that family extends farther than just blood or marriage, there are so many we consider family that do not technically fall into those two categories. We find family as a deep connection to others and sometimes you may consider others more of family than your own flesh and blood. But, we are all a part of one big family as children of God.

As a part of something way bigger than ourselves, God's purpose for us all, we need to lean into these relationships that we have to help each other fulfill our purposes and become the greatest version of ourselves. God places people in your life to not only help guide you, but to help you grow and learn. There are always opportunities to help others or be helped from others, and both are blessings given to you.

You need to surround yourself with people on the same mission as you, each one being their extraordinary selves living out their calling and purpose from God. You need a tribe that sharpens you, encourages you, and challenges you. One that shares your values and supports your mission. That's the essence of Extraordinary Strength Method™: relational strength fueled by a common purpose.

Matthew 18:20 (ESV) says, "*For where two or three are gathered in my name, there am I among them.*"

Together, there is true strength when you have a humble spirit and lift each other up and help carry each other's yokes. Don't run away from the fear or the challenge if it is too big for you. Charge into it with all that you have with those that are around you and you can take on anything. We are made to go through this life together and help each other out, it is how we all become extraordinary.

Life is designed to be lived in unity with others. God created us for community, not isolation. While serving others is vital, humility is also required to accept help when we need it. The strength of relationships often grows through overcoming challenges together, sharpening one another as iron sharpens iron. Surround yourself with people who support your growth, and remember: true strength is found in facing life's challenges together with God and the people He places in your life.

When we gather in unity, God moves. When we support one another, we grow stronger together. When we charge forward into life's battles with others by our side, we become unstoppable.

Reflection Questions

- What challenge are you currently facing that you've been trying to handle alone? Who could you invite into it?

- Are you more comfortable serving others or receiving help? Why?

- Who in your life has lifted you up during adversity? Have you thanked them or shared how much it meant?

- Are you carrying your weight in relationships, or expecting others to carry yours?

- Do you have a circle of people who sharpen you and align with your mission? If not, how can you start building that?

- Who could benefit from your encouragement or support this week?

- Are there relationships that need mending or more intentional investment?

- What's one step you can take this week to walk in unity and relational strength?

Habits to Build: Strength in Unity

- Embrace Humility
  - Practice receiving help with grace, not guilt.
- Serve with Joy
  - Look for opportunities to bless others daily.
- Invest in Relationships
  - Prioritize connection and quality time.
- Be Vulnerable
  - Share your burdens in safe, trusted spaces.
- Evaluate Your Circle
  - Surround yourself with people on a mission aligned with your values.
- Be a Family Builder
  - Treat others like family, especially those who need encouragement.
- Practice Gratitude
  - Regularly affirm and appreciate your inner circle.

Bringing it Together: Unity in Action

- The next time someone offers to help—pause before declining. Accept it and express gratitude. Remind yourself: your humility may be their blessing.

- Identify one person this week you can serve with no strings attached—through a kind gesture, words of encouragement, or lending a hand. Let it come from joy, not obligation.

- Reach out to someone important you haven't connected with lately—call, message, or spend time together.

- Write down a current challenge and share it with a trusted friend or mentor. Let others into your battle so they can stand with you.

- Evaluate your five closest relationships—do they support your spiritual growth? If not, seek out one new relationship aligned with your purpose—join a group, community, or mentorship.

- Reach out to someone who feels alone. Offer prayer, time, encouragement, or simply spend time with them. Be the family they need today.

- Write down one person each day this week you're thankful for—and tell them why.

Final Charge: Strengthen the Circle, Sharpen the Spirit

You were never meant to walk this journey alone. Strengthen your spirit by strengthening your circle. Show up for others. Let them show up for you. This is how we grow. This is how we overcome it. This is how we become extraordinary—together.

Let go of the pride that keeps you isolated. Accept the help God sends your way. Step into relationships that sharpen, stretch, and strengthen you.

Living in unity, charging into life's challenges together, and lifting one another up is how we all become extraordinary and live out the purpose God has called us to.

Because when you surround yourself with those who walk in purpose and faith, you don't just survive—you thrive.

As we've just explored, unity isn't just about receiving support—it's about building it, together. While charging into life's challenges side by side sharpens your spirit, it's the ongoing relationships we maintain that truly sustain us. That brings us to a critical yet often overlooked element of spiritual strength in today's world: your social fitness.

Together, we rise. Together, we grow. Together, we become extraordinary.

Let's go.

Pillar 4: Strength in Relationships—Social Fitness for the Spirit

We are not meant to go through this life alone—but in today's world, many feel like they are. Despite constant digital "connection," society faces what's now called a loneliness epidemic. In 2023, U.S. Surgeon General Dr. Vivek H. Murthy released a powerful advisory titled Our Epidemic of Loneliness and Isolation, revealing how deeply this crisis is impacting our well-being:

"People began to tell me they felt isolated, invisible, and insignificant... Loneliness is far more than just a bad feeling—it harms both individual and societal health... The mortality impact of being socially disconnected is similar to that caused by smoking up to fifteen cigarettes a day… But we have the power to respond."

This epidemic affects the mind, body, and spirit—and it's calling for a new kind of fitness: social fitness.

Social fitness means intentionally investing in meaningful relationships that uplift you and align with your God-given purpose. It's more than simply being around people—it's about cultivating connection that strengthens your spirit.

So in a world that is more "connected" than ever due to social media and the internet, people are more isolated and lonely than ever, creating even more health issues through mind, body, and spirit. Dr. Vivek H. Murthy's writings cover how it negatively affects individuals and communities as a whole. All of this points toward the fact that you and the rest of the world need more social connections and relationships with others to live out a healthy and purpose filled life.

What Is Social Fitness?

Social fitness is the spiritual and relational counterpart to physical and mental strength. It's your ability to build, maintain, and navigate healthy, life-giving relationships with others. It includes:

- Emotional Support: Having people who help buffer stress and keep you grounded.

- Belonging: Feeling truly seen, heard, and accepted.

- Growth: Engaging in conversations that challenge, inspire, and help you grow.

At its core, social fitness includes:

- Social Skills: Communication, empathy, active listening, and conflict resolution.

- Social Awareness: Reading the room, respecting boundaries, and being present.

- Relationship Management: Trust-building, maintaining healthy boundaries, and showing support.

- Support Network: Surrounding yourself with people who encourage your growth in faith, fitness, and life.

Why It Matters for Your Spirit

Social fitness is spiritual fitness. Why? Because God didn't create us to be isolated—He created us for community. And as part of the Extraordinary Strength Method™, this is a spiritual discipline just as essential as training your body or mastering your mind.

Many people gather together, but few connect deeply. Too often we stop at surface-level conversation—weather, sports, shows— never diving into the meaningful discussions that nurture the soul. True connection often lies just past the awkwardness. That first uncomfortable moment can be the gateway to conversations that heal, grow, and transform.

You don't need to fix someone to be a great friend. Just be present. You do not have to completely agree with what someone is saying or even have advice for them, but being the person that truly listens to them to hear them can make a world of difference in someone's life. Many times there is no response needed or even wanted, just a hug or a hand on the shoulder letting them know you care.

Listen with your full attention. Offer a safe space. A hug. A prayer. That's where relational strength begins.

Social Fitness is Like Training

Just like strength training requires effort, intentionality, and consistency—so do relationships. Some days it's easier to isolate, scroll, or stay on the surface. But when you choose to engage and go deeper, your spirit grows stronger.

Building social fitness takes:

- Discipline—showing up even when it's inconvenient.
- Vulnerability—being willing to open up.
- Encouragement—uplifting others as you walk through life together.

It's not about being perfect—it's about being present.

The Extraordinary Strength Method™ in Action

Relationships are central to becoming the extraordinary you. In our method, Spiritual Strength is not developed in isolation—it's formed in community. Every rep of meaningful conversation, every act of listening, every time you show up for someone or let them show up for you—you're building spiritual muscle.

Whether it's a church small group, a fitness community, or a close circle of friends who push you to be better, these relationships are part of your calling. They're the people God has placed in your life to help shape you—and for you to shape in return.

Just as your body thrives through movement, your spirit thrives through connection. And just like you plan your workouts and nutrition, you must also plan time to strengthen the relationships that support your spirit.

Reflection Questions

- How strong and meaningful are your current social connections? Are they nourishing your spirit—or leaving you empty?

- Do you tend to open up more easily, or is it easier for you to listen to others? Why?

- Who consistently encourages and uplifts you? How can you invest more into that relationship?

- Are there any relationships in your life that need healing or strengthening?

- Do you make regular time for relationship-building, or do you let "busyness" get in the way?

- What fears hold you back from pursuing deeper connections? How can you begin to face those?

- Are you surrounding yourself with people who support your growth—physically, mentally, and spiritually?

- What step can you take this week to deepen one meaningful relationship in your life?

Habits to Build: Strength in Relationships

- Prioritize Meaningful Connection
  - Be intentional about nurturing relationships that fuel your spirit.

- Move Past the Awkwardness
  - Get comfortable with discomfort to create real connection.

- Be an Active Listener
  - Truly hear others without planning your reply.

- Strengthen Your Support Network
  - Surround yourself with people who elevate your walk with God and your life mission.

- Create a Social Fitness Routine
  - Treat social time like your workouts—it's part of your health.

- Be a Source of Encouragement
  - Speak life regularly into those around you.

- Step Outside Your Comfort Zone
  - Stretch your relational limits by forming new connections.

- Reduce Digital Distractions
  - Be fully present in your in-person interactions.

- Engage in Acts of Service
  - Serve others to strengthen connection and community.

- Practice Gratitude for Relationships
  - Cultivate thankfulness for the people God has placed in your life.

Bringing it Together: Social Fitness in Action

- Schedule one meaningful conversation this week with someone you care about—go deeper than the surface.

- Ask a thoughtful question like "What's bringing you joy?" or "What's been challenging you lately?"

- In your next conversation, put your phone away and reflect back what you hear to show presence.

- Make a list of 3–5 people who pour into your life. Reach out to one of them this week to invest in the relationship.

- Block time each week for connection—small groups, dinners, phone calls, or shared workouts.

- Send one encouraging message, prayer, or note of appreciation each day this week.

- Join a new group, attend a faith/fitness event, or introduce yourself to someone you've been meaning to connect with.

- Keep your phone out of sight when meeting with someone—practice full focus.

- Offer practical or emotional help to a friend this week. Even small acts of service can deepen trust.

- Write down one person you're thankful for each night and why. Let them know.

As we've seen throughout this cornerstone, our spirit is not strengthened in isolation—it grows in unity, community, and meaningful connection. But it also flourishes in clarity. As we draw these spiritual pillars together, this final charge is your call to action. Just as you train your body and renew your mind, you must also commit to strengthening your spirit with intention and discipline. This is where everything begins to align—your faith, your gifts, your relationships, and your purpose. This is where the Extraordinary You begin to take shape.

Final Charge: Strengthen the Ties That Strengthen You

Just as you train your body for strength and endurance, and your mind for focus and resilience, you must also train your spirit for connection, compassion, and calling. Social fitness, like every pillar of the Extraordinary Strength Method™, requires effort, discipline, and consistency. We are not meant to walk this journey alone. God created us for connection—both to uplift others and to be uplifted ourselves. Social fitness is not optional for an extraordinary life—it's essential.

The loneliness epidemic is real, but you don't have to be a part of it. You have the power to forge deeper relationships, move beyond surface-level interactions, and build meaningful bonds that strengthen your Mind, Body, and Spirit. It starts with small, intentional reps: showing up, listening, reaching out, and making space for real conversations.

The quality of your relationships directly impacts the quality of your life—and your ability to live out your God-given calling. Are you training this area of your life with the same urgency you train your body or pursue your goals?

Social fitness isn't a luxury—it's a requirement for the extraordinary life God is calling you to live. Like all great things, it's worth the work. Step into the challenge. Embrace the awkwardness. Build the relationships that will sharpen your spirit and strengthen your mission.

Because at the end of the day, true success, deep joy, and lasting meaning aren't found in what you achieve, but in who you share the journey with. This is how you rise. This is how you grow. This is how you become the extraordinary you God has made you to be.

So, take the next rep in this training. Build stronger ties. Be present. Speak life. Let people in.

Because your growth, your calling, and your mission will never be fully realized in isolation.

You were made to rise—and you were made to rise together.

And now—surrounded by the strength of others, grounded in faith, and filled with spiritual fuel—you are ready to take the next step: discovering your why. Because God didn't just create you for connection... He created you for purpose.

Let's talk about passion. Let's talk about purpose. Let's talk about what truly makes you unstoppable.

Let's go.

Pillar 5: Strength in Passion & Purpose

> *"And we know that for those who love God all things work together for good, for those who are called according to his purpose." – Romans 8:28 (ESV)*

"When your passion meets your purpose, you become unstoppable." – Martin Rooney

Passion without direction can burn out. Purpose without passion can feel lifeless. But when both are fueled by the Spirit of God and aligned with your unique gifts, you step into the unstoppable strength of your calling.

Just like physical strength is built through training, and mental strength is built through discipline, your spiritual strength is built when your passion becomes aligned with purpose. This is the Essence of the Extraordinary Strength Method™—bringing the mind, body, and spirit into alignment so that your purpose is not just something you believe in... it's something you live.

What Is Passion?

Passion is more than excitement—it's a fire in your bones. Passion is defined as a "strong and barely controllable emotion" and "an intense desire or enthusiasm for something." It reflects the God-given spark inside you. Intense and barely controllable. Powerful ways to define and describe what everyone should be looking for within their lives.

Can you imagine what the world would be like if every person was filled with passion about their God given purpose?! I think we see a world today that gets passionate about the wrong things, though. Our world often fuels passion toward temporary things—money, fame, comfort—and not toward our eternal purpose.

The result? People burn bright for the wrong things and burn out. But godly passion, aligned with your spiritual identity, never fades—it endures, even through adversity.

> *"Make your enthusiasm for success stronger than your fear of failure and you will become unstoppable." – Martin Rooney*

True Enthusiasm Comes From the Spirit

Along with being an intense desire, being passionate means you have to be enthusiastic about your purpose. The word enthusiasm comes from the Greek word *enthousiasmos*, meaning "to be inspired or possessed by God." In other words, enthusiasm is evidence that you are filled with the Spirit.

True enthusiasm comes from being in God, to be filled with His spirit! For so many, enthusiasm only comes when things are going well for them and get more of an immediate gratification for what they are doing. But when things get tough, does the enthusiasm stay or does the fear of failure stop you? Unless you are driven by something more than the instant gratification, if you have a passion for your purpose, fear of failing will hold you back. When you are filled with spirit from God for His purpose for your life, enthusiasm should be a given. That no matter the challenges that are going on, your passion and enthusiasm drive you through.

When you pursue your purpose with enthusiasm, you're not relying on adrenaline—you're relying on anointing. That's the difference between worldly hype and kingdom fire. When you're filled with Spirit-driven enthusiasm, your mindset shifts from "I have to do this" to "I get to do this for God!"

This is a core tenet of the Extraordinary Strength Method™: cultivating spiritual drive that sustains you through both mountaintop moments and valley seasons.

> *"Whatever you do, work heartily, as for the Lord and not for men, knowing that from the Lord you will receive the inheritance as your reward. You are serving the Lord Christ." – Colossians 3:23-24 (ESV)*

Your passion, enthusiasm, and your purpose are deeper than just things of this world. Knowing that you are making an impact on others lives and fulfilling your calling from God with the knowledge of the inheritance God has promised you in His kingdom.

Fuel That Doesn't Fade

Even with great passion, there will be days when enthusiasm fades, doubt creeps in, or you question whether you're making a difference. That's when you must return to the source—not your goals, not your grind, but your God. In those times, look to Christ for guidance and discernment. His spirit will fan the flame and reignite your passion. You have victory in Him!

> *"But thanks be to God, who gives us the victory through our Lord Jesus Christ. Therefore, my beloved brothers, be steadfast, immovable, always abounding in the work of the Lord, knowing that in the Lord your labor is not in vain." – 1 Corinthians 15:57-58 (ESV)*

When you live by the Spirit, your extraordinary strength doesn't come from hustle—it comes from hope. You may not always feel on fire, but the Spirit can always reignite what He started in you.

During those days that it seems that you are not making a difference, remember that God has called you into something more. You may not see it now, but there is something greater happening and you are a part of the story. Your labor is not in vain. Let your enthusiasm, passion, and purpose lead to the extraordinary you that God has called you to be!

Your Why = Your Fuel

Your *why* is the deep reason behind what you do. It's the purpose that gives direction to your passion.

Without it, you chase distractions. With it, you live intentionally.

Your *why* helps you:

- Rise above fear and failure.
- Stay committed when comfort calls.
- Make bold decisions for God's glory.
- Push through pain and pressure.
- Live with joy, gratitude, and focus.

The Extraordinary Strength Method™ calls this purpose alignment— the point where mind, body, and spirit unite toward something greater than self.

You are part of something greater than yourself. Even on the days you feel discouraged, remember—your labor is not in vain. Stay passionate, remain enthusiastic, and trust that God is leading you to the extraordinary.

Reflection Questions

- What is my God-given purpose, and am I pursuing it passionately?

- What excites me, stirs my heart, and reflects God's heart for the world?

- When enthusiasm fades, where do I turn to reignite my spirit?

- Am I more afraid of failure or more in love with my calling?

- How can I align my daily actions with my deepest purpose?

Habits to Build: Strength in Passion & Purpose

- Clarify Your Purpose
    - Spend intentional time reflecting and praying over your God-given calling.

- Fuel Your Passion Daily
    - Surround yourself with spiritual inputs—Scripture, mentors, music, books—that ignite your why.

- Cultivate Enthusiasm
    - Begin each day with spiritual reminders that your work is for the Lord, not man.

- Defeat Fear of Failure
    - Recall past victories where God carried you through and use them to fuel present courage.

- Make an Impact Beyond Yourself
    - Let your passion serve others—look for daily ways to inspire and encourage.

- Stay in the Word

  - Build your foundation on Scripture to stay grounded in truth and aligned with your purpose.

- Practice Gratitude

  - Use gratitude as fuel. Reflect on daily blessings that keep your spirit encouraged.

Bringing it Together: Passion & Purpose in Action

- Write down what you believe God is calling you to do. Revisit and refine it weekly.

- Start your day with prayer or worship—set your focus on serving the Lord, not people.

- Journal moments when God showed up in your past. Let those memories silence your doubts.

- Send one text, message, or voice note of encouragement each day—share your fire.

- Highlight Scripture verses that affirm your calling and post them where you'll see them often.

- Each night, write down three things you're grateful for, especially related to your calling.

- Ask yourself each day, "Who can I serve or inspire today with what God's given me?"

You are not here by accident. You are here on assignment.

God has planted passion in you, not for popularity or fleeting excitement—but for purpose. And that purpose is fueled by the Spirit, anchored in truth, and ignited by your why. You're meant to live with fire, fueled by the Spirit, grounded in truth, and aimed toward something eternal.

When passion aligns with purpose, you don't just survive—you thrive. You don't just push through—you rise up. Even when enthusiasm fades, the Spirit will fan the flame again.

So lean into your calling. Let your passion burn bright. Let your purpose guide every step. And never forget—your labor is never in vain.

Let your *why* ignite the extraordinary you God created you to be.

Because when your passion meets your purpose, you become unstoppable.

Let's go.

Pillar 6: Strength in Your *Why*–Aligning Purpose With Action

Every person is created with a purpose, a calling that is uniquely theirs. But purpose alone isn't enough—it must be fueled by passion and enthusiasm, grounded in faith, and aligned with God's will. This is your *why*—the deep reason behind everything you do.

Your *why* is the fire that wakes you up with urgency. It's the deeper meaning behind your work, your relationships, your health, your habits, and your faith walk. A strong *why* will:

- Give your life direction.
- Keep you moving forward when challenges arise.
- Help you stay focused on what truly matters.
- Allow you to serve and impact others.
- Be greater than money, status, or comfort.
- Take care of your Mind, Body, and Spirit.
- Keep you rooted in purpose through the storms of life.

This is the essence of the Extraordinary Strength Method™: living intentionally by anchoring your mindset, physical health, spiritual life, and purpose into something greater than yourself. Without a clear *why* you will be pulled in different directions by worldly distractions. But with a clear *why*—rooted in Christ—you become anchored, focused, and unshakable.

Purpose Turns Motion Into Mission

Purpose gives life direction and meaning. It transforms daily living from randomness into intentional action for something greater. Every person is born with a unique purpose and gifts from God, but many fail to recognize their potential for greatness. Unfortunately, in today's world, many are passionate about the wrong pursuits—wealth, status, and temporary pleasures—while neglecting their true God-given purpose.

Our world is full of people who are passionate—but about the wrong things. Corporations are passionate about profits. Influencers are passionate about fame. But passion alone, when disconnected from purpose, becomes chaos. As followers of Christ, our passion must be greater than the world's pursuit of profit. Our mission must be clearer than the noise of distraction.

> *"Those who love money will never be satisfied by it."* – Ecclesiastes 5:10 (ESV)

True contentment comes from living out your calling, serving others, and trusting that God has placed you exactly where you need to be.

Purpose-driven living requires thoughtful time management and the courage to face fear and uncertainty. Colossians 3:23-24 calls us to "work heartily, as for the Lord and not for men" because our ultimate reward is from Him. This means that our passion, enthusiasm, and purpose are bigger than any earthly measure of success.

The Work of Purpose: Discipline and Alignment

Living with purpose isn't automatic. It takes thoughtful planning, bold action, and the courage to say no to comfort in favor of calling.

The Extraordinary Strength Method™ teaches that aligning your Mind, Body, and Spirit starts with your *why*. Every decision—from how you train your body, to how you spend your time, to how you respond to difficulty—is filtered through that greater mission.

- Your mind stays sharp because your thoughts are guided by vision, not circumstance.

- Your body stays disciplined because health is part of honoring the temple God gave you.

- Your spirit stays fueled by faith, because you're working for something bigger than success—you're working for eternity.

God has given you 86,400 seconds every day. Use them with intention. Don't bury your talents in fear or comfort. Like in the Parable of the Talents, you're called to invest what God has given you—and take bold, faithful action.

Health and faith are foundational to living out one's purpose. Neglecting these areas makes it difficult to fulfill God's calling. Many allow life's busyness and circumstances to dictate their actions, leading them to postpone their physical and spiritual well-being. But ignoring these pillars only leads to burnout, dissatisfaction, and an inability to serve others effectively.

The contrast is clear: Purposeful living results in greater joy, healthier relationships, and meaningful contributions to the world. Conversely, living without purpose leads to dissatisfaction, poor health, and spiritual emptiness.

To step into the extraordinary version of yourself, you must take action. Reflect on what you've always felt called to do. Identify your passions. Envision the person God created you to be. And most importantly, take the first step—because there is no perfect time other than right now.

By identifying your why and trusting God's guidance, you can align your mind, body, and spirit to become the extraordinary version of you that God created you to be! We will dive more into the entirety of purpose in Cornerstone 4.

Test It. Take Action. Trust God.

Your *why* becomes clearer with movement. Don't wait for the "perfect time." Start small. Serve someone. Try something new. God often reveals the next step in motion—not in waiting.

Even when the flame flickers, remember: God will never abandon you.

"*Your labor is not in vain.*" – 1 Corinthians 15:58 (ESV)

"*What do you think? If a man has a hundred sheep, and one of them has gone astray, does he not leave the ninety-nine on the mountains and go in search of the one that went astray? And if he finds it, truly, I say to you, he rejoices over it more than over the ninety-nine that never went astray.*" – Matthew 18:12-14 (ESV)

Reflection Questions:

- What do I feel deeply passionate about?

- How has God uniquely gifted me to serve others?

- What struggles or experiences have shaped my purpose?

- When do I feel most alive and fulfilled?

- What step can I take today to live more in line with my *why*?

Habits to Build: Strength in Your Why

- Define Your Why in Writing
    - Reflect regularly on your God-given purpose and passions. Write them down and revisit them weekly.

- Start with God Daily
  - Begin each morning with Scripture and prayer, asking for clarity and strength to live out your purpose.

- Filter Decisions Through Purpose
  - Ask, "Does this align with my why?" before committing your time, energy, or resources.

- Protect Your Priorities
  - Say no to distractions that don't serve your mission. Purposeful living requires intentional boundaries.

- Strengthen Your Temple
  - Prioritize physical health as an act of stewardship—move daily, eat to fuel, rest to restore.

- Fuel with Faith
  - Anchor yourself in God's promises through consistent time in His Word. Let Scripture guide your direction.

- Take Faithful Action
  - Even when you feel uncertain, take the next right step. Movement reveals clarity.

Bringing it Together: Purpose in Action

- Write your personal mission statement. Keep it visible—on your mirror, desk, or phone.

- Schedule time weekly to reflect on whether your current habits align with your purpose.

- Replace one distraction this week (social media, TV, etc.) with 15 minutes of spiritual or physical growth.

- Choose one area of health (mind, body, or spirit) to recommit to as a reflection of your purpose.

- Identify one act of service or step of obedience you've been delaying—and do it this week.

- Make a "Why List" of 5 reasons why your calling matters. Read it when motivation fades.

- Surround yourself with others who are mission-driven. Join a group, community, or mentorship aligned with your purpose.

Final Charge: Anchor to Your Assignment

Your *why* isn't just about you. It's about how God wants to use you for His greater glory.

You were created on purpose, for a purpose—and your why is the compass that keeps you moving in the right direction. It is the fire beneath your discipline, the reason behind your resilience, and the anchor that holds when life's storms rise.

But even the strongest purpose can fade when it's not protected. That's why God calls us not just to know our why, but to live it daily—with boldness, faith, and consistency.

You are not meant to drift through life reacting to circumstances. You are meant to lead your life through intention and action, driven by a God-given mission greater than yourself.

So today, take the next step. Start where you are. Do what you can. Trust that God will guide your every step as you move forward in faith.

Because when your why is rooted in Christ, no obstacle can stop you. No fear can hold you back. No failure can define you.

You are aligned. You are called. You are becoming the extraordinary you.

The Final Call: Living in the Spirit

Becoming the Extraordinary You Through a Spirit-Led Life

You've now walked through the journey of Awakening Your Spirit—a journey rooted in serving others, bearing the Fruit of the Spirit, leaning into the strength of unity, building meaningful relationships, and aligning passion and purpose. But there's one truth that unites them all:

You can't live an extraordinary life by human strength alone.

Each of these pillars flourishes through the power of the Holy Spirit. He is the source. The strength. The sustainer.

To live an extraordinary life, you must live a Spirit-led life.

The Spirit is the thread that weaves together everything in this cornerstone:

- It is the Spirit that empowers you to serve when you're tired.
- It is the Spirit that produces love, joy, peace, and all the fruit that transforms you.
- It is the Spirit that humbles you enough to accept help and lifts you to help others.

- It is the Spirit that strengthens your social fitness and builds meaningful connections.

- It is the Spirit that fans into flame your passion and aligns it with your purpose.

- And it is the Spirit that gives you the clarity and conviction to live out your why.

The Consequences of Misalignment

Understanding the cost of spiritual neglect is just as important as understanding the reward of spiritual strength. This is where many get stuck—strong in one area, but empty in another. Let these truths serve as both a warning and a wake-up call:

- Strong Mind but Weak Body = Vision Without Execution

    - You know the plan. You dream big. But without physical strength, your vision stays stuck in your head—never taking shape in reality..

- Strong Body but Weak Mind = Action Without Direction

    - You're constantly in motion. You hustle hard. But without a focused mind, you're running fast… in the wrong direction.

- Strong Mind and Body but Weak Spirit = Burnout and Emptiness

    - On the outside, you look successful. You're focused. You're driven. You're fit. But on the inside, you're drained. Your motivation feels hollow. Your energy fades quickly.

This is what happens when your spirit is underdeveloped—when you try to sustain your strength through willpower alone instead of Spirit-power.

That's why Cornerstone 3: Awaken Your Spirit is essential.

This section gave you what was missing:

- A deeper "why" for your service.

- The Fruit of the Spirit to guide your character.

- A renewed dependence on your community.

- Passion that's rooted in something eternal.

You've shifted from self-reliance to Spirit-alignment. You've begun living from overflow instead of exhaustion.

A Recap of Your Spirit Training—Extraordinary Strength Method™ in Action:

Pillar & Spiritual Strength Habit

- Pillar 1: Serving Others
    - Live generously without expectation of return
- Pillar 2: Fruit of the Spirit
    - Cultivate love, joy, peace, patience, kindness, goodness, faithfulness, gentleness, self-control
- Pillar 3: Strength in Unity
    - Embrace interdependence; allow yourself to be lifted by others when needed

- Pillar 4: Strength in Relationships
  - Build deeper social connections through vulnerability, presence, and encouragement
- Pillar 5: Strength in Passion & Purpose
  - Fuel your actions with enthusiasm rooted in God's calling
- Pillar 6: Strength in Your why, Your Purpose
  - Let your purpose be bigger than yourself and guided by God's voice and timing

Final Reflection

- How has my understanding of spiritual strength grown through these chapters?
- Which pillar of the Spirit do I feel strongest in? Which one needs more growth?
- Where do I see the Fruit of the Spirit showing up in my relationships and choices?
- Am I trying to live alone, or am I living in a Spirit-led community?
- How can I carry these Spirit-based practices into my next season of purpose?

Key Habits for Living in the Spirit

- **Practice Spiritual Presence**—Begin and end each day with quiet reflection or prayer, inviting the Spirit to guide you.

- **Serve with Love, not for Recognition**—Check your motives. Let every act of service be Spirit-led, not self-led.

- **Pursue Connection, Not Perfection**—Stay engaged with your community and social fitness, even when it's messy.

- **Let the Fruit Be the Evidence**—Focus more on who you are becoming than what you are achieving.

- **Refuel with the Spirit Daily**—You can't pour from an empty cup. Rest, worship, pray, and reconnect regularly.

Final Charge: Lead with the Spirit, Live with Power

Living in the Spirit means living with divine purpose, passion, and power. The Spirit empowers us to serve others, overcome fear, and grow in community. He equips us to bear the fruits of the Spirit, which reflect God's love to the world. The Spirit strengthens our resolve, renews our enthusiasm, and fuels our passion to fulfill the calling God has placed on our lives.

The Spirit is not an accessory to your faith. He is the fuel.

He strengthens you when you're weak.

He anchors you when you feel lost.

He fans the flame when your fire begins to fade.

When we live by the Spirit, we are unstoppable. The Spirit is not just an abstract idea or force; He is the life-giving power of God working in us every day. When we live by the Spirit, our lives are filled with purpose, passion, and perseverance. Through the Spirit, we are equipped to face life's challenges, fulfill our God-given calling, and experience the victory that is ours in Christ Jesus.

When you live by the Spirit, you are no longer operating in your own strength—you are being led by God Himself. That's how ordinary people step into extraordinary lives.

So don't stop here.

Don't settle for spiritual awareness—walk in spiritual authority.

Don't just believe in your calling—live it with boldness and power.

Because this is only the beginning.

What's Next: Now, the Journey Turns Toward Your Purpose

Awakening your spirit was never meant to be the end—it's the preparation for what comes next.

As you live in the Spirit, you become more in tune with God's voice and more aware of the calling placed on your life. You've strengthened your heart, refined your character, embraced humility, and built meaningful connections. Now, it's time to discover what all of that has been preparing you for.

It's time to step boldly into your God-given purpose. Because a strong mind, body, and spirit mean nothing if they're not put to use for something greater. And you were made for something greater.

Your purpose isn't something you chase. It's something you step into. And the time to step in is now.

You've been prepared. You've been refined. You've been filled.

Now it's time to live on *purpose*.

Because here's the final truth:

All Three Without Purpose = Strength Without Impact

You can have a sharp mind, a strong body, and even a sensitive spirit— but if you don't know why you're here, you'll drift.

You'll build a castle on sand. You'll grow but never bear fruit. You'll inspire but never truly transform.

Your purpose is the final piece. It's the target for your training, the direction for your growth, and the mission behind your strength.

Now, let's forge your purpose. Cornerstone 4 begins now.

Let's go.

Forging Your Purpose

You've done the inner work—strengthening your mind, sharpening your body, and awakening your spirit. You've confronted lies, overcame fear, deepened your faith, and built a solid foundation in who God says you are. But this transformation wasn't just for your benefit. It was preparation. Now, it's time to take everything you've built and pour it into the world around you. This is the moment where faith meets action, where passion fuels purpose, and where you begin to live externally what God has forged in you internally. It's time to stop searching and start walking boldly in the life you were created for. The extraordinary you have been awakened—now it's time to live on mission.

Pillar 1: The Power of Purpose

When the Fight Fades

I watched my mom lose her sense of purpose after cancer. And it was almost as devastating as the disease itself.

Before the diagnosis, she was full of life, driven by her passions and responsibilities. But after all that she went through, something unexpected happened—she felt lost. All that she had worked for throughout her career was now gone since she was not able to go back to work. Mom was diagnosed with stage 4 lung cancer and was put on permanent disability. For the first year or so, my mom had purpose in her fight, but that could only last so long.

At first, the fight itself gave her purpose. It was her mission. But when the battle became less about surviving and more about enduring, that purpose started to slip away. The treatments ended, but the struggles didn't—and without something to fight for, she felt lost. Medications upon medications made her extremely lethargic and low energy. She struggled to get up and move around each day. But, after two years of surgery's, treatments, and setbacks, it actually got worse–the cancer had metastasized to her brain and she needed brain surgery.

The doctors gave her six months. Maybe less.

She heard them. She nodded.

Then, without hesitation, she made her decision.

Challenge accepted.

It gave my mom something to fight for again. The struggle of low energy and being lethargic continued after the surgery due to the amount of medications she was on, though. So about three months after that surgery, my mom and I were sitting down talking as we did at least once a week, and we were talking about her quality of life. I did not like seeing my mom this way and she agreed that she did not want to live this way. We knew there were risks of her stopping the medications, but we discussed that life was about quality, not quantity. I told her I was for her stopping the medications, and she responded "oh good, because I stopped taking them two weeks ago." We laughed together and then started to try to come up with a plan of what quality of life will look like for her. She was ready to live—not just survive.

I wish I knew then what I know now, because I feel I could have helped my mom a lot more. I knew little of purpose and how it is so life giving. By God's grace, though, I was able to help my mom find some purpose in life by helping her take amazing trips to see places she always wanted to go. It gave her something to look forward to and a purpose to continue her fight. It wasn't enough, though. The day to day drained her physically and mentally, not knowing what to do and what she was truly living for. By sheer will and grit, my mom outlived every prognosis. She fought harder and longer than anyone expected. Looking back, I can see the little bits of purpose she had that drove her to continue to fight: the trips with her family, my wife and I getting married, and the birth of her first grandchild, my daughter.

Unfortunately, after my daughter was born, my mom did not have much fight left. She passed nine months after my daughter was born. She survived nine years after her initial diagnosis. That experience taught me something powerful: without purpose, even the strongest will fades.

Purpose isn't just about staying alive—it's about having something worth fighting for.

What is Purpose?

Purpose is more than a nice idea or an inspiring quote on a wall. It is the compass that gives your life direction. It transforms random actions into intentional living. It answers the deepest human question: Why am I here?

Purpose is the reason for which something exists. It is your why behind the what. The foundation beneath every meaningful action. Without it, life becomes reactive. With it, life becomes driven.

Most people are searching for purpose without realizing they were created with one from the very beginning. Ephesians 2:10 (ESV) says:

> *"For we are His workmanship, created in Christ*
> *Jesus for good works, which God prepared*
> *beforehand, that we should walk in them."*

That means your life isn't random. Your story isn't accidental. God created you with intentional design—for impact, for meaning, and for mission.

Marin Rooney says, "*The tragedy in life is not that people don't have greatness inside of them, the tragedy is that people often don't recognize it.*"

I want to help you discover your greatness, uncover your true purpose, and take the necessary steps to fulfill it. That's why we need to uncover your extraordinary purpose, because when we do, everything changes.

Why Purpose Changes Everything

So why does purpose matter so much?

Because without purpose, you'll drift. Without purpose, you'll burn out. Without purpose, you'll chase things that leave you empty.

But when you discover your *why*—the thing God created you for—everything changes. It gives you energy on hard days. It brings meaning to your struggles. It becomes the reason you get up in the morning and the reason you keep going when life gets hard.

This isn't just a mindset thing. Purpose changes how you think (*Mind*), how you care for your health (*Body*), and how you connect to God and others (*Spirit*). That's why it's the foundation of everything we've talked about so far—and why it's the launching point for what comes next.

Purpose in the Extraordinary Strength Method™

In the Extraordinary Strength Method™, purpose is not the end—it's the beginning. It's the *why* behind all three previous cornerstones:

- Master Your Mind—Purpose gives your thoughts direction and helps you overcome limiting beliefs.

- Strengthen Your Body—Purpose motivates discipline in your health, fitness, and habits.

- Awaken Your Spirit—Purpose connects your service and faith to a higher calling.

Purpose is what ties the entire method together. It gives your mental, physical, and spiritual training deeper meaning. You don't just build strength for the sake of it—you build strength so you can *serve, lead, endure, inspire,* and *impact.*

When you train with purpose, health becomes a calling. Discipline becomes joy. Service becomes legacy. And *that* is when you begin to forge the extraordinary you.

Reflection & Journal Prompts

Take a moment to reflect deeply on what drives you:

- Do I currently feel like I'm living with purpose—or just going through the motions?

- What experiences in my life have most shaped how I view my calling?

- When have I felt most alive, most energized, most fulfilled?

- Who or what am I fighting for each day—and is it aligned with God's design for me?

- If I truly believed God created me for a reason, how would I live differently starting today?

Habits to Build: A Purpose-Filled Life

- Start Your Day with Purpose
  - Begin each morning by reconnecting with your why through prayer or journaling.

- Create Purpose-Driven Goals
  - Align your goals with your God-given purpose instead of worldly success.

- Anchor Purpose in Scripture
  - Meditate on Bible verses that affirm your value and calling.

- Reflect Regularly
    - Make space to revisit your purpose and check your alignment weekly.
- Live with Legacy in Mind
    - Make decisions through the lens of long-term impact rather than temporary reward.

Bringing it Together: Living with Purpose in Action

Purpose isn't just something you think about—it's something you live.

- Each morning, write one sentence that defines your current purpose and identify a specific way to live it out that day.

- Revisit your current goals and ask, "Does this serve the mission God has for me?" Make adjustments where needed.

- Memorize and meditate on Ephesians 2:10 daily to remind yourself that your life is God-designed for impact.

- Set aside weekly time (10–15 min) to ask: "Am I living aligned with my why?"

- Filter your major decisions through the question: "Will this matter five years from now? Is this who I'm called to be?"

When you act from your why, everything gains new meaning—your workouts, your work, your relationships, your rest. Even struggles become sacred when it's endured for a greater purpose.

Your strength isn't just for you—it's meant to serve, inspire, and lead others. And that begins with choosing to live every day on purpose.

Final Charge: Let Purpose Fuel Your Fight

Purpose is the bridge between your potential and your impact. It's the fire that keeps you going when motivation fades, and it's the reason you rise after every setback. It's your anchor, your compass, and your fuel.

It's what helps you endure when life hurts.

It's what brings light to your darkest days.

It's what gives your strength meaning.

Without it, even the strongest will crumble. But with it, even the weakest can stand tall.

You were created with purpose, by a God who doesn't make mistakes. He designed you with intention—to love, to lead, to serve, and to bring light into the lives of others.

Now is your time to live like that's true.

Not someday. Today.

Because when you live with purpose, you become unstoppable.

Let's continue this journey—by facing the barriers that threaten to steal your why. Let's overcome the distractions of time and fear... and step into the mission God has placed on your life.

Because purpose isn't just something you believe in—it's something you must defend every day.

Let's go.

Pillar 2: Time, Fear, and Purpose

"So teach us to number our days, that we may
get a heart of wisdom." – Psalm 90:12

Time—The Currency of Purpose

"Imagine you had a bank account that deposited $86,400 each morning. The account carries over no balance from day to day, allows you to keep no cash balance, and every evening cancels whatever part of the amount you had failed to use during the day. What would you do? Draw out every dollar each day!

We all have such a bank. Its name is Time. Every morning, it credits you with 86,400 seconds. Every night it writes off, as lost, whatever time you have failed to use wisely. It carries over no balance from day to day. It allows no overdraft so you can't borrow against yourself or use more time than you have. Each day, the account starts fresh. Each night, it destroys any unused time. If you fail to use the day's deposits, it's your loss and you can't appeal to get it back.

There is never any borrowing time. You can't take a loan out on your time or against someone else's. The time you have is the time you have and that is that. Time management is yours to decide how you spend the time, just as with money you decide how you spend the money. It is never the case of us not having enough time to do things, but the case of whether we want to do them and where they fall in our priorities."

You are given 86,400 seconds every single day. They cannot be carried over. You don't get to invest them and watch them grow later. You either use them with purpose—or they're gone. The difference between the extraordinary and the ordinary lies in how those seconds are spent.

The question is: are you spending your time aligned with your God-given purpose, or are you simply letting the days pass by?

Time is the most valuable resource you have. Every second is an opportunity—to serve, to love, to grow, to lead, to become. But so often, we allow time to slip through our fingers, consumed by distractions, procrastination, or fear.

You don't need more time—you need more clarity about your why.

When your purpose is clear, time becomes sacred. You start making decisions that reflect where you're going instead of where you've been. And that's what separates a purpose-driven life from a passive one.

Fear—The Barrier to Purpose

Fear is one of the greatest enemies of purpose. It doesn't always show up loudly. Sometimes it whispers:

What if I fail?

What if they don't believe in me?

What if this isn't the right time?

Fear causes hesitation, and hesitation kills momentum.

In Matthew 25, Jesus shares the Parable of the Talents—a master gives his servants different amounts of money. Two of them invest and multiply what they've been given. One buries it out of fear. When the master returns, he praises the ones who took bold action. But the one who let fear stop him? He is called "wicked and lazy."

God did not give you gifts to bury. He gave you gifts to multiply.

Every purpose-driven life will encounter fear. But faith is what separates those who act anyway. When you realize your time is limited and your calling is eternal, you stop letting fear call the shots.

Many let their circumstances dictate their behaviors and actions. This happens in their career, relationships, health, and faith. We start thinking that 'this is not the time' and 'it's too risky' for something like that right now.

So if not now, then when?

There is never going to be a perfect time for anything in our lives. When we feel that calling is placed on our hearts, we are being called by God and I promise you it will definitely not feel like the timing is right. But it's not about our timing, it's about His and it's about obeying Him.

We don't have to have it all together. God does not call the qualified, he qualifies the called. When called, the perfect time is now. God will match your passion and your purpose and lead you to the extraordinary, but we have to listen and take action.

Fear of failure, fear of judgment, and fear of the unknown keep people from stepping into their God-given purpose. But when you trust in God's plan and move forward in faith, you overcome fear and begin to walk in your true calling.

Purpose Over Profit—The Right Measure for Success

One of the biggest misconceptions people have about purpose is that it's tied to how much money they make. We live in a world that constantly equates success with wealth, status, and possessions. But if that were true, why do so many high-earning, highly successful people feel empty?

Fulfillment isn't found in a bank account—it's found in pursuing your God-given mission.

Now, let's be clear: There's nothing wrong with financial success. You can—and should—work toward financial stability and success. But when money becomes the purpose instead of a byproduct of serving your purpose, something critical is lost.

Ecclesiastes 5:10 (NIV) warns,

> *"Whoever loves money never has enough;*
> *whoever loves wealth is never satisfied with*
> *their income. This too is meaningless."*

Money can buy comfort, but it can't buy meaning. It can buy distractions, but it can't buy fulfillment. Money is a tool, not a purpose.

The true measure of success isn't your income—it's your impact. Are you changing lives? Are you using your gifts for something bigger than yourself?

The Extraordinary Strength Method™ teaches us to align our Mind, Body, and Spirit in pursuit of divine purpose. That alignment helps us resist the world's definition of success and embrace God's instead.

You were created for something far greater than comfort or status. You were created to make a difference—and when you begin using your time with purpose and walking in faith, the extraordinary begins to unfold.

The Extraordinary Strength Connection

Let's anchor this pillar to the Extraordinary Strength Method™:

- Mind (Mental Strength): Refuse to let fear run your thoughts. Train your mind to focus on God's promises over your insecurities. Renew your mind daily with truth and vision.

- Body (Physical Strength): Energy is required to carry out your purpose. Time spent on your health is an investment in your mission.

- Spirit (Spiritual Strength): Faith over fear. Prayer over panic. Presence over pressure. The Holy Spirit is your power source when time feels short and fear feels heavy.

Reflection Questions

- How am I currently spending my 86,400 seconds each day?

- What is one fear that keeps holding me back from living with purpose?

- Am I measuring success by profit or by impact?

- What would my life look like if I invested my time as if my purpose truly mattered?

- What's one talent God has given me that I've been "burying?" What step can I take to start using it?

Habits to Build: Using Time & Facing Fear with Purpose

- Start with the End in Mind

  - Each morning, acknowledge the value of your 86,400 seconds and set a daily intention aligned with your purpose.

- Prioritize What Matters Most

  - Schedule your time around your God-given mission— not distractions or demands.

- Confront Fear with Truth

  - Write down common fears and speak Scripture over them to remind yourself of God's promises.

- Invest Time in What Fuels You

  - Protect time for your spiritual growth, physical health, and mental renewal daily.

- Choose Obedience Over Delay

  - Take action on your calling now—don't wait for the "perfect time." Build the habit of saying yes in the face of fear.

Bringing it Together: Time and Fear in Action

- Audit Your Time

  - Track how you're spending your hours for seven days. Highlight any areas where time is leaking away from your purpose and restructure accordingly.

- Make a Fear List

  - Identify one fear that's holding you back from taking action. Then choose one small step of faith to confront it this week.

- Replace Fear with Scripture

  - Write down three Scriptures to declare when fear creeps in. Keep them somewhere visible—on your mirror, phone, or dashboard.

- Act On One Buried Talent

  - Ask yourself: What's one ability or idea I've been sitting on? Set a seven-day challenge to put it to use in service of someone else.

- Redefine Success

  - Every Sunday, journal how you've made an impact that week—not based on money or status, but on meaning, service, and obedience.

Final Charge: Redeem the Time, Overcome the Fear

Time is the currency of your calling. Fear is the tax that tries to steal it.

You've been given a gift—86,400 seconds a day to move closer to who God created you to be. But that gift can be wasted through hesitation, fear, or distraction. The world will always offer excuses. Your calling offers something better: impact.

Don't bury your gifts. Don't let fear silence your voice. Don't wait until you "have time. You have time right now.

God doesn't wait for perfect people or perfect timing. He moves through the bold, the faithful, and the available.

So take the step. Speak the truth. Make the call. Write the message. Share the story.

Use your time with urgency. Face your fear with faith.

And watch purpose unfold through every moment you choose obedience over delay.

Because when you master your time and defeat your fear, your purpose becomes unstoppable.

Your purpose requires all of you—mind, body, and spirit—working in unity.

Misalignment between these core areas is often what keeps people stuck. You may know your calling, but if your energy is low, your thoughts are overwhelmed, or your faith is running on empty, you'll struggle to move forward.

That's why alignment is essential.

In the next pillar, we'll explore how to bring your mind, body, and spirit into sync—so you can walk in strength, clarity, and confidence as the extraordinary version of you that God created you to be.

Let's go.

Pillar 3: Aligning Mind, Body, and Spirit with Your Purpose

If your purpose is *the why* behind your life, then alignment is *the how* that makes it sustainable.

So many people struggle with living out their calling not because they lack purpose, but because they're out of sync. Their mind is anxious and overwhelmed. Their body is exhausted and neglected. Their spirit is disconnected from God. And when even one piece is off, everything else begins to wobble.

The Cost of Misalignment

Maybe you've felt it:

- You want to live with purpose, but your thoughts are clouded with self-doubt or fear.

- You have passion, but your body doesn't have the energy to sustain the work.

- You believe in God's calling, but you're running on empty spiritually.

Alignment is not about perfection—it's about integration. It's about your entire being moving in the same direction. When your mind, body, and spirit are aligned with your purpose, you move with clarity, confidence, and power.

> *"Though one may be overpowered, two can defend themselves. A cord of three strands is not quickly broken."* – Ecclesiastes 4:12 (NIV)

In the same way, your life becomes unshakable when your mind, body, and spirit are woven together with purpose at the center.

Now, some have never actually taken time to figure out what their purpose truly is. Our society is known for just shuffling people to the next thing and telling them what they should do in life. When you were in school, have you ever been asked what you wanted to do for the rest of your life?

Many of us had some big dreams in the beginning; playing a pro sport, inventing something amazing, finding the cure to a disease, and many other truly great things. But how many of us were told that it's not realistic and it won't happen? That we need to be more realistic and pick a real job that we can be safe in and provide for our future families?

I know I was told that by my family and by my teachers. We get scared that our dreams are just that and we can never make them come true. So we settled. We pick the safe route.

But your dreams and calling from God should scare you. If trying to make that come true doesn't scare you, it's not big enough. Any great calling by God will bring in some fear, but only with God can we make it happen. The safe route is not the calling and purpose God has placed on you.

It is easy to pick the safe route, though. We tell ourselves we will be more comfortable there and that we will be happy there. But truly that is why people are depressed, anxious, and dissatisfied with their lives. They are not doing what truly fulfills them.

But when people are unsure of what to do for their future as they go to graduate high school, they do what so many told us to do; go to college and get a degree in something that brings in a decent income and has job opportunities, instead of pursuing something they are passionate about. Then they get stuck in a job they dislike and try to make a little bit of time on their days off for what they are truly passionate about.

No wonder so many are depressed. Working Monday through Friday doing something they don't like just so they can try to make time on Saturday to do something they enjoy, and then resent Sunday because the next day they have to go back to the job they aren't fulfilled by.

Home life is hard because you are always in a bad mood due to work, your relationships with people are strained and you want to be alone more often, you have no desire to take care of your health because you always feel drained, and you don't see the reason behind it all, so you have a hard time believing in God. You are in and out of the doctor's office being put on a slew of medications for depression, anxiety, and health related issues. You buy more things thinking it will fill the void you have but nothing seems to satisfy. Recipe for disaster.

Now imagine what life would be like if you were living with passion and purpose. Most days of the week, you truly love what you are doing and get excited when you wake up because you get to go and do that. Your energy is higher which gives you the drive to do more things in your life and take care of your health and fitness which brings you even more energy and joy since you have the health to do all the things that you want. You are rarely at the doctors' and on little to no medications because of your healthy habits. You come home most days in a great mood, which leads to a happy home life and happy relationships. You create more experiences with those you care about instead of purchasing more material things. Now this is more like it!

We all have gifts that we were given by God and a purpose greater than just ourselves. We all need to use those gifts and pursue our calling and purpose so we may live a fulfilling life and become the extraordinary people that God has made us to be.

Don't miss that finding and fulfilling your purpose is directly correlated to your health. You can't live your purpose if you are too unhealthy to do so. We think that we can put it to the side for a while and just 'grind' on our work and purpose, but trust me, I've been there and done that and it does not go well.

Many people allow circumstances to dictate their lives. They wait for the "right time" to pursue their purpose, yet that time never comes. The truth is, there is no perfect moment—the time to act is now.

If purpose is what drives us, then we have to ask: Why do so many people struggle to find it?

One of the biggest reasons people feel lost is because their mind, body, and spirit are misaligned.

- Their mind is filled with doubts, limiting beliefs, and fear.
- Their body lacks the energy, strength, and resilience to take action.
- Their spirit is disconnected from faith, gratitude, and meaning.

Without all three working together, purpose feels unclear, distant, and unreachable.

Remember the Unified Vision of Strength:

- **Mind**: The foundation that shapes everything else.
- **Body**: The vehicle that executes what the mind envisions.
- **Spirit**: The power source that sustains both mind and body.
- **Purpose**: The direction that gives meaning to all three.

Alignment is only powerful when it's anchored in purpose.

Mind: Your Beliefs Drive Your Behavior

Your thoughts shape your actions. If your mindset is filled with doubt, anxiety, or limiting beliefs, it will be nearly impossible to live purposefully. You'll stay stuck in cycles of procrastination, perfectionism, or fear.

This is the cost of a strong body but a weak mind: You're busy and active, but directionless. It's action without clarity. You confuse motion for progress and wonder why you feel aimless despite doing so much.

But when your mindset is built on faith, discipline, and confidence, you become unstoppable. This is why *Mastering Your Mind*—the first cornerstone of the Extraordinary Strength Method™—is foundational. Aligning your thoughts with truth allows you to act in alignment with God's calling.

Mastering Your Mind isn't just about resilience—it's about thinking clearly so you can live on purpose.

Ask yourself: What is one limiting belief you need to replace with God's truth?

Body: Your Health Is the Vehicle of Your Purpose

You can have the greatest vision in the world—but if your body is worn down, sick, or depleted, you won't have the stamina to carry it out.

This is the cost of a strong mind but weak body: You dream big, you believe deeply, but you can't act. You're stuck with vision but no execution. Frustration builds as your body fails to support what your mind knows is possible.

Neglecting your physical health doesn't just impact you—it limits your ability to serve others, stay energized, and walk in excellence. Stewarding your body is not a vanity project—it's a spiritual discipline. That's why *Strengthen Your Body* is the second cornerstone in the Extraordinary Strength Method™.

A strong body supports a strong purpose. A tired body will eventually undermine even the clearest purpose.

Strengthening your body fuels your purpose with energy and resilience—it's not vanity, it's stewardship.

Ask yourself: Is your current level of physical health helping you or hindering you in your pursuit of purpose?

Spirit: Fueling Your Purpose with Faith

Your spirit is the anchor that keeps you rooted in the *why* behind what you do. A disconnected or neglected spirit leads to burnout, discouragement, and aimlessness.

This is the cost of a strong mind and body but weak spirit: You have the mindset and the habits, but no eternal anchor. You burn out chasing productivity without peace. You achieve, but still feel empty. Without the Spirit, all your strength eventually collapses under pressure.

But a spirit that is awake and alive in Christ gives you peace, clarity, and fire for the mission ahead.

Through *Awaken Your Spirit*—the third cornerstone—we've learned how critical spiritual strength is for enduring life's trials and living in service to something greater than yourself. When your spirit is aligned with God's will, you stop chasing empty success and start walking in true significance.

Awakening your spirit means staying filled, led, and empowered—so your purpose stays God-centered, not self-centered.

Ask yourself: Are you regularly filling your spirit with God's Word, prayer, and connection?

The Extraordinary Strength Method™ in Full Alignment

The Extraordinary You isn't created through shortcuts—it's forged through intentional alignment. When your mind believes, your body acts, and your spirit trusts, you begin living from your purpose—not just chasing it.

The cost of mind, body, and spirit without purpose is this: Strength without impact. You may be impressive—but not impactful. You look strong on the outside, but your energy has no direction. You were created for more than performance—you were created for purpose.

This is what The Extraordinary Strength Method™ is all about:

- *Mental strength* to stay focused and courageous.
- *Physical strength* to execute your mission with energy and discipline.
- *Spiritual strength* to stay grounded and guided by truth.

When all three are aligned with purpose, your life becomes a powerful testimony of what God can do through someone fully surrendered to His purpose.

Once your mind, body, and spirit are aligned with purpose, you're no longer living on autopilot—you're finally positioned to live with deep intention and clarity. But alignment alone isn't the destination. It's the launching point.

Reflection Questions:

- Where do I feel the most out of alignment—my mind, body, or spirit?

- What's one small step I can take today to begin realigning that area?

- How would my life look if all three were working together toward one purpose?

- What's holding me back from full alignment, and how can I surrender that to God?

Habits to Build: Aligning Mind, Body, and Spirit for Purpose

Alignment is only powerful when it's anchored in purpose. These habits are not just about self-discipline—they are about living intentionally in every area so you can carry out your God-given mission. Each habit is designed to keep your mind, body, and spirit aligned with the Extraordinary Strength Method™—so that purpose becomes not just your direction, but your lifestyle.

Mind – Align Thoughts With Purpose

- Daily Mental Recalibration

  - Start each day by asking: What matters most today in light of my purpose? Journaling or reading Scripture can help renew your mindset and re-center your thoughts.

- Affirm with Truth

  - Speak life over yourself with affirmations rooted in God's promises, not your doubts. Let your thoughts be fueled by faith, not fear.

- Purposeful Inputs

  - Fill your mind with content that strengthens your calling—limit comparison and media that distracts you from your purpose.

- Cornerstone Connection

  - Mastering Your Mind isn't just about resilience—it's about thinking clearly so you can live on purpose.

Body – Steward Energy for Purpose

- Train With Intention

  - Move your body not just for aesthetics, but to maintain the physical capacity to carry out your mission—whether that's leading, serving, creating, or enduring.

- Fuel for the Mission
  - Eat and rest in ways that support longevity and stamina, so you have energy to do what God is calling you to do every single day.

- Respect Your Limits
  - Overwork and burnout dishonor your temple. Build in recovery so you can continue to show up strong for the long haul.

- Cornerstone Connection
  - Strengthening Your Body fuels your purpose with energy and resilience—it's not vanity, it's stewardship.

Spirit – Stay Anchored in the Source of Purpose

- Start with Surrender
  - Begin your day by inviting the Holy Spirit to align your heart with God's will. Pray, listen, and ask for divine clarity.

- Revisit Your Why in Worship
  - Make space in your week to reconnect with why you're doing what you're doing. Worship shifts the focus from pressure to presence.

- Guard Your Heart
  - Protect your spirit from discouragement by staying in God's Word, surrounding yourself with life-giving people, and staying rooted in gratitude.

- Cornerstone Connection

  - Awakening Your Spirit means staying filled, led, and empowered—so your purpose stays God-centered, not self-centered.

Bringing it Together: Alignment in Action

Alignment isn't a one-time decision—it's a daily commitment to live intentionally with your mind, body, and spirit working together toward God's purpose for your life. These action steps are how you live that alignment, not just in thought, but in real, tangible, purposeful movement.

Mind in Action – Train Your Thoughts for Purpose

- Set a Daily Intention Rooted in Purpose

  - Each morning, write down one way your thoughts will support your purpose today—whether that's courage in a conversation, focus on your work, or grace toward yourself.

- Replace a Limiting Belief With Truth

  - Identify one thought that has been holding you back, and write out a Scripture or truth to replace it. Speak it aloud daily until it becomes your new default.

- Curate Your Mind's Diet

  - Choose one source of distraction (negative media, comparison, toxic input) to remove this week, and replace it with a podcast, devotional, or book that strengthens your purpose.

Body in Action – Move and Fuel With Mission in Mind

- Anchor Your Workouts to Your Why

  - Before each training session this week, take 30 seconds to mentally connect your workout to your mission. Remind yourself: "I train to serve, lead, and live fully."

- Optimize One Habit That Supports Energy

  - Choose either your sleep, hydration, or nutrition and set a small goal that enhances your energy. For example: Go to bed 30 minutes earlier or prep lunch with whole foods 3x this week.

- Schedule Recovery as a Non-Negotiable

  - Choose one rest practice (Sabbath, stretch session, slow walk, unplugged evening) and schedule it on your calendar as a commitment to your long-term purpose.

Spirit in Action – Stay Connected to the Source

- Begin Each Day With Spiritual Alignment

  - Before grabbing your phone, pause to pray or journal. Ask God: "Align my spirit with your purpose today. Show me where to go, what to say, and who to serve."

- Create a Weekly Worship Check-In

  - Set aside one block of time (Sunday morning, midweek evening, etc.) to reflect: Am I still aligned with my why? Am I pursuing God's purpose or drifting from it?

- Serve From Overflow, Not Obligation
  - Choose one way to serve this week that energizes your spirit—whether it's encouraging a friend, volunteering, or helping someone with no strings attached. Let it remind you why you're here.

Final Charge: Live in Alignment, Live on Mission

You were not created to live compartmentalized—where your mind says one thing, your body does another, and your spirit is barely holding on. You were created to live whole, aligned, and on fire for your calling.

When you align your mind, body, and spirit with God's purpose, your life becomes an unstoppable force for good.

Let this be your charge:

- Don't settle for survival when you were made for significance.
- Don't accept misalignment when you were created for power and peace.
- Don't confuse busyness for fruitfulness—purpose requires alignment.

You now have the framework. You've built your strength. You've heard the call.

Now go live it—aligned, activated, and anointed.

The world doesn't need more noise. It needs more aligned, purpose-driven warriors. And that starts with you.

Now it's time to activate everything you've built so far and connect it to something greater—your why.

Your why is the fuel behind the action, the fire that keeps your purpose alive when life gets hard, and the deeper reason that makes your health, discipline, and faith more than just habits—they become a mission.

Let's go.

Pillar 4: Find Your Why, Live Your Why

> *"He who has a why to live can bear almost any how."—Viktor Frankl*

> *"The two most important days in your life are the day you are born and the day you find out why."—Mark Twain*

You've built strength. You've aligned your life. Now it's time to channel that strength and alignment into action that has eternal impact.

Purpose gives life direction and meaning. It transforms daily living from randomness into intentional action for something greater. Every person is born with a unique purpose and gifts from God, but many fail to recognize their potential for greatness. Living purposefully isn't about accumulating wealth but about fulfilling a calling and positively impacting others' lives.

Purpose-driven living requires thoughtful time management and the courage to face fear and uncertainty. Pursuing purpose often requires taking risks, pushing past comfort zones, and trusting God's timing. Health and faith are foundational to living out one's purpose. Neglecting these areas makes it difficult to fulfill God's calling.

Purposeful living results in greater joy, healthier relationships, and meaningful contributions to the world. Conversely, living without purpose leads to dissatisfaction, poor health, and spiritual emptiness.

By identifying your passions and trusting God's guidance, you can align your mind, body, and spirit to become the extraordinary version of you that God created you to be.

Your *why* is the driving force behind your God-given purpose. It's the deeper reason behind your daily choices, your habits, your sacrifices— and ultimately, your legacy. It's what makes all the discomfort and discipline worth it.

But here's the truth:

Many people never find their *why* because they never stop to ask the right questions. They stay in survival mode, checking boxes, going through the motions, hoping someday they'll feel fulfilled. Someday never comes—unless you intentionally pursue it.

Your *why* is already inside of you. God placed it there before you were born.

> *"Before I formed you in the womb I knew you, before you were born I set you apart." – Jeremiah 1:5 (NIV)*

Your job is to uncover it, live it, and let it shape every area of your life.

Finding Your Why Begins with Faith

Your *why* isn't something you randomly stumble upon—it's something you *prayerfully uncover*. It's a divine calling tied to your gifts, your pain, your passions, and your past. It's the combination of what breaks your heart, what fuels your joy, and what God has uniquely wired you to do for others.

Ask yourself:

- What would I do even if I never got paid for it?
- What makes me feel alive?
- What do I feel burdened or called to fix in this world?
- What have others consistently told me I'm gifted at?
- How has my pain prepared me to serve someone else?

These aren't small questions. But they lead to big answers.

Your Why Is the Anchor for Your Extraordinary Life

Without a strong why:

- Discipline won't stick.
- Health goals will fade.
- Spiritual routines will feel empty.
- Fear will win.

But *with* a strong why? You become *unstoppable*.

When your why is connected to God's calling, the hard days become meaningful. The sacrifices become sacred. The journey becomes filled with purpose.

> *"Whatever you do, work at it with all your*
> *heart, as working for the Lord, not for human*
> *masters." – Colossians 3:23 (NIV)*

Your why is your worship.

Forging Your Why Through Action

You don't just *find* your why. You live your way into it.

- Write it down. Speak it out loud. Refine it over time.

- Surround yourself with the right people. People who help you remember your mission when you forget.

- Take small steps each day. Your purpose is too big to be lived in one moment—it's built through daily faithfulness.

- Return to God. When you lose clarity, go back to the Source. His voice will reignite the fire within you.

Your Life with a Clear *Why*

- You wake up with energy and direction.

- You stop chasing status or approval.

- You say *no* to distractions and *yes* to divine purpose.

- You take care of your health because your mission needs you strong.

- You stop waiting for the perfect time and start showing up fully, now.

Reflection Questions

- What makes me come alive—mentally, physically, and spiritually?

- What has God placed on my heart to fix, serve, build, or bring into the world?

- What burden or passion keeps resurfacing that I haven't fully acted on yet?

- Who am I uniquely positioned to serve because of my story, pain, and gifts?

- In what ways have I allowed fear, fatigue, or distractions to silence my why?

- If I fully embraced my why today, how would my choices change this week?

- How can I better align my mind, body, and spirit with my divine purpose?

Habits to Build: Live Your Why

These habits anchor your God-given purpose into your daily life. The goal is not just to find your why, but to *live* it—through faith, discipline, and intentional action.

- Start Each Day With Your Why
  - Begin every morning by speaking or writing your purpose out loud. Remind yourself what you're living for before distractions have a chance to define your direction.

- Reflect Weekly on Your Mission
  - Schedule a weekly check-in with God to revisit your why. Ask: "Am I still aligned with what You've called me to do?"
- Serve With Intention
  - Look for one way each week to use your gifts in service of others. Whether through encouragement, mentoring, creativity, or generosity—your purpose will grow stronger through action.
- Say No With Purpose
  - Create a habit of eliminating distractions or opportunities that don't align with your mission. A purposeful "no" protects a meaningful "yes."
- Steward Your Health as Fuel for Mission
  - Prioritize sleep, training, and nutrition—not for vanity, but because your mission requires your energy and strength to endure.

Bringing It Together: Living Your Why in Action

Living your why means applying it to every area of your life—mind, body, and spirit—so your purpose isn't just something you believe in, but something you become through daily decisions.

Mind in Action – Direct Your Thoughts Toward Purpose

- Journal your "why" each morning as your internal compass for the day.

- Replace negative self-talk with mission-driven declarations like: "I am called. I am equipped. I am becoming who God created me to be."

- Eliminate one mental distraction this week that is pulling you away from your calling.

Body in Action – Build the Energy to Carry Your Mission

- Move your body with your mission in mind—train to serve, not just to look a certain way.

- Meal prep one day this week with the mindset: "My purpose needs my strength."

- Prioritize one recovery habit (sleep, stretching, unplugging) so your energy remains consistent and sustainable.

Spirit in Action – Keep God at the Center of Your Why

- Begin each morning with a short prayer: "Lord, guide my steps in alignment with the purpose You gave me."

- Fast from something that's cluttering your spiritual clarity (e.g., social media, negative input).

- Attend church, serve in your faith community, or initiate a spiritual conversation to stay mission-minded and grounded in truth.

Final Charge: Live Your Why Every Day

Your why isn't just a motivational slogan. It's a calling from God that demands action. When your why is grounded in Him, nothing can stop you—not fear, not failure, not fatigue.

It is the reason you are still breathing.

It is the fire that fuels your discipline, your strength, and your service.

It is the anchor that steadies you when life tries to knock you off course.

Without your why, your strength becomes self-serving.

With your why, your strength becomes sacred.

So today, decide:

Will you keep drifting through life, hoping meaning finds you?

Or will you rise with intention, rooted in purpose, and walk boldly toward your calling?

Your purpose is already planted inside of you.

It's time to water it with action.

Live your why.

Lead with your gifts.

Love with your strength.

And leave a legacy that echoes into eternity.

This is the path of the Extraordinary.

This is the life you were created to live.

So what are you waiting for?

Step into your calling.

Live your why.

Become the extraordinary you God created you to be.

Let's go.

The Final Call: The Extraordinary Life in Action

This is the activation of everything you've built. The final step in forging your purpose is to live it boldly, daily, and intentionally.

> *"Do not merely listen to the word, and so deceive yourselves. Do what it says." – James 1:22 (NIV)*

This is it. The moment everything comes together.

You've clarified your purpose. You've discovered your why. You've aligned your mind, body, and spirit.

Now it's time to put it all into action.

Because here's the truth: Purpose without action is just potential.

An extraordinary life isn't something you stumble into—it's forged day by day through intentional living. The extraordinary version of you is already within you… but it must be *activated.*

> *"So also faith by itself, if it does not have works, is dead." – James 2:17 (ESV)*

Living a life of purpose isn't just about *knowing* your calling—it's about *walking* in it every single day.

What Does Extraordinary Life Look Like?

It's not a perfect life. It's not a life without failure or fear.

It's a life of consistency, courage, conviction, and compassion. It's a life lived on mission—not for your own glory, but for God's.

You're not chasing titles, trends, or trophies. You're chasing impact, integrity, and influence for the Kingdom.

It looks like:

A Renewed Mindset—One grounded in belief, discipline, gratitude, and faith. You've silenced self-limiting beliefs, embraced fear as fuel, and replaced excuses with empowered choices. You lead your thoughts, instead of letting them lead you.

A Strengthened Body—One treated as a temple, not a trophy. You train not for vanity but for vitality. You fuel it with intention so you have the energy to serve, lead, and love deeply. Your physical strength supports your life's mission.

An Awakened Spirit—One alive with service, humility, and deep connection. You live by the Fruit of the Spirit, invest in relationships, walk in community, and let your faith anchor you through storms and celebrations alike.

A Forged Purpose—One that aligns every action with a higher calling. You know your why and live it daily. Your habits aren't random; they're reflections of your mission. You measure success by impact, not applause.

When these are fully aligned, you stop drifting and start living intentionally. You no longer wake up dreading the day—you rise with energy because you know you're walking in God's design.

But remember:

Strong Mind but Weak Body = Vision Without Execution

Strong Body but Weak Mind = Action Without Direction

Strong Mind and Body but Weak Spirit = Burnout and Emptiness

All Three Without Purpose = Strength Without Impact

The extraordinary life isn't about perfection—it's about alignment. When you unite your mind, body, spirit, and purpose, you become the unstoppable, extraordinary you that God created you to be.

Reflection Questions

- What's one small action I can take today that aligns with my purpose?

- Where in my life am I waiting instead of walking?

- Am I truly living the habits of the extraordinary me?

- Who am I serving—and how is that fulfilling my purpose?

- What would my life look like if I lived each day as though it were on purpose?

Habits to Build: The Extraordinary You

The *extraordinary life* is built with ordinary habits, done with extraordinary purpose.

- Start Your Day With Purpose
    - Every action either pulls you closer to your calling or further from it. Choose wisely. Begin each morning by asking, "How can I live on purpose today?" Don't just plan tasks—align them with your purpose.

- Move with Mission

  - Treat your body like the vessel of your purpose. Train for strength, fuel it with intention, and rest to restore. Extraordinary strength isn't built overnight—it's forged through discipline and discomfort.

- Protect Your Mindset

  - Speak truth over your life daily. Reject fear, comparison, and distraction. They will try to steal your purpose. Guard your thoughts. Renew your mind in God's Word.

- Stay Rooted in Relationships

  - Cultivate meaningful connections with people who challenge, sharpen, and uplift you. An extraordinary life is lived in *connection*.

- Practice Purposeful Service

  - Look for ways to lift others with small, consistent acts of service—especially when it's inconvenient. You were not made to serve *yourself*. Purpose multiplies when it's shared.

- Revisit Your Why Often

  - Keep your why visible. Let it guide your decisions, your boundaries, and your daily actions. Knowing your why is only half the battle—living it is where transformation happens.

Bring it Together: The Extraordinary Life in Action

Now is the time to fully activate The Extraordinary Strength Method™ in your life:

- Master Your Mind—Choose belief over doubt, focus over distraction, and discipline over comfort.

- Strengthen Your Body—Honor your body as the temple and tool God has given you for His work.

- Awaken Your Spirit—Stay connected to your source—through prayer, Scripture, service, and worship.

- Forge Your Purpose—Align your life with the mission God placed inside you. Your life is not random. It's divinely intentional.

Practical Steps to Activate Your Purpose:

- Morning Mission Check

  - Write your daily mission statement each morning. It can be one sentence or one word that keeps you focused on purpose.

- Weekly Purpose Planner

  - Schedule time every Sunday to reflect on how you're living out your purpose—spiritually, mentally, and physically. Adjust where needed.

- Health as Worship

  - Build non-negotiables into your week for movement, meal prep, and recovery. These are not distractions—they are divine preparation.

- Mentor & Serve
  - Find someone to mentor or encourage this month. Your purpose multiplies when it's poured into someone else.
- Keep a "Why Wall"
  - Create a space (physical or digital) where you keep reminders of your calling: photos, verses, goals, and stories that reflect who you're becoming.
- Take Bold Action
  - Identify one area where you've been hesitating. Take one bold step this week in obedience to the purpose God placed in your heart.

Final Charge: Step Into the Extraordinary Life

This is your moment.

You've built the foundation. You've renewed your mind, strengthened your body, awakened your spirit, and uncovered your purpose.

Now comes the part that matters most—living it.

It's time to put it all into action—daily, consistently, faithfully.

Remember:

- A strong mind alone gives you vision, but without a strong body, that vision stays stuck in your head.
- A strong body alone gives you action, but without a focused mind, you move without meaning.

- A strong mind and body together without a strong spirit will drive you to burnout and emptiness.

- Even if you have all three, without purpose, your strength is wasted—it makes no eternal impact.

The world needs the extraordinary version of you—and God is calling you to rise.

An extraordinary life is not marked by perfection, but by purpose in motion.

It's forged through small, faithful steps.

Every rep. Every meal. Every thought. Every prayer. Every act of service. Every choice.

Let it all be a reflection of the extraordinary life He's called you to live.

It's built by showing up when it's hard, by saying yes to God when it would be easier to say no, and by serving others even when it costs you something.

You are not called to be average.

You are called to be extraordinary.

The world needs your light. Your family, friends, community, and future generations need the fully activated, extraordinary version of you.

You're not here to merely exist. You're here to transform.

So rise. Step into your calling. Live your why.

Take the first step.

Then the next.

And keep walking—on purpose, with strength, and for the glory of God.

Become the extraordinary you God created you to be.

Let's go.

Step Into the Extraordinary You

Embrace the Journey You've Walked

You've made it. You've walked through the full Extraordinary Strength Method™—Mastering Your Mind, Strengthening Your Body, Awakening Your Spirit, and Forging Your Purpose. That's no small task. Most people go their entire lives never doing the deep work you've done here. So pause, reflect, and fully acknowledge how far you've come.

You've walked through the fire—through mindset shifts, physical discipline, spiritual awakening, and the forging of purpose. This wasn't just a casual read or a feel-good message. This was a journey—through pain, passion, reflection, and transformation.

You've explored who you are, why you're here, and what it takes to become the person God created you to be. You've gained tools, truth, and a renewed sense of hope. And most importantly, you've stepped into a new identity—one not based on the world's expectations, but rooted in eternal purpose.

You've shown up for yourself in a world that constantly demands your attention but rarely calls you to greatness. But you didn't settle. You committed to uncovering the extraordinary version of you—and you've done more than just scratch the surface. You've dug deep. You've wrestled with big questions. You've taken action.

Most people never do that. But you did.

And now?

You are stronger.

Not just in muscle or mindset—but in spirit, in purpose, and in your capacity to impact the world around you.

Remember the Mission

You were not created to live an ordinary life.

You were created on purpose, with purpose, for a purpose. God has equipped you with unique gifts, experiences, and strengths—many of which have been uncovered and sharpened throughout this journey. Your mission is not just about becoming the best version of yourself—it's about becoming the version of you that God had in mind when He formed you in the womb.

This book was never just about personal development. It was about spiritual alignment. Your growth is meant to glorify God, serve others, and create a ripple effect of impact through your family, your community, and the world.

Remember: extraordinary strength isn't just what you build—it's what you give. Your mission now is to live it out, boldly and unapologetically.

Commit to the Path

Becoming extraordinary doesn't happen in a week—or even in the time it took to read this book.

Extraordinary strength is not a destination; it's a lifelong commitment. It's built brick by brick, one habit, one prayer, one rep, one act of service at a time. And there will be setbacks. There will be seasons where motivation fades, energy dips, and the path feels unclear. But that's when your commitment matters most.

When the emotions wear off, discipline must take over. When life gets chaotic, your cornerstones will guide you back.

This isn't about perfection—it's about persistence. Keep showing up. Keep building your mind, your body, and your spirit. Keep pursuing your purpose with passion. Even when no one's watching. Especially when no one's watching.

Because strength built in private becomes power revealed in public.

Living the Extraordinary Life

You've walked the path through mind, body, spirit, and purpose—the four cornerstones of the *Extraordinary Strength Method*™. This isn't just a framework; it's a way of life. And now, the challenge is to live it out.

Let's revisit what you've built.

You mastered your mind—confronted fear, took responsibility, and adopted the mindset of a warrior. You learned that belief, discipline, gratitude, and perseverance are not traits you're born with; they're muscles that grow through training. You've seen how mental strength is the foundation that shapes your reality and your future.

You strengthened your body—not for vanity, but for vitality. You committed to training, fueling, and stewarding your body so it can support your calling. You discovered that physical strength sharpens mental toughness and fuels energy for service. You don't just move better—you live better.

You awakened your spirit—by aligning your life with God's truth and becoming part of something bigger than yourself. You grew in faith, built community, and embraced the power of relationships. You learned that spiritual strength doesn't come from being perfect, but from abiding in God's presence, bearing fruit, and letting Him guide your path.

And finally, you began forging your purpose. You dug deep into your why, examined your time, conquered fear, aligned your life, and committed to a path of intentional action. You've seen how purpose transforms ordinary living into extraordinary impact. And now, you've been given the tools to step into it fully.

But this book was never the finish line—it's just the launching point.

You are equipped. You are empowered. You are capable of more than you can imagine. And most importantly: you are called.

Called to live with courage.
Called to lead others.

Called to rise again when life knocks you down.

Called to become the extraordinary you God created you to be.

So now, ask yourself:

- Which cornerstone needs the most attention in your life today?

- What small step will you take to strengthen it?

- Who will you become when you commit to this path?

Don't wait for the perfect time. Don't wait to feel ready. Start where you are, with what you have, and trust that God will meet you there.

This is your moment.

This is your mission.

This is your extraordinary life in action.

Prayer & Commissioning Statement: A Call to Rise

Heavenly Father,

Thank You for the one reading this right now. Thank You for walking with them through every page of this journey—the highs and lows, the conviction and encouragement, the truth and transformation.

Lord, You knit them together with a purpose far greater than comfort or status. You made them strong—not just in body, but in mind and spirit. I pray right now that You would ignite in them a holy fire. A passion for truth. A hunger for righteousness. A relentless pursuit of the calling You've placed on their life.

When the enemy whispers doubt, remind them of who they are in You.

When the world offers comfort, give them the courage to choose growth.

When the road gets hard, remind them that they do not walk alone.

Let them walk forward in boldness.

Let them live with discipline and joy.

Let them serve with passion and humility.

Let them rise again, and again, and again—because You, Lord, never leave or forsake them.

And now, I commission them:

To live with purpose.

To lead with faith.

To train with discipline.

To love without limits.

To embody the strength of mind, body, and spirit that glorifies You.

Let their life be a testimony.

Let their legacy be one of impact.

And let their strength be extraordinary—not by their power, but by Yours.

In Jesus' name, Amen!

Final Charge: Step Into the Extraordinary

You were not created for mediocrity. You were not called to live stuck, numb, or drifting.

You were created in the image of God—with purpose, with power, and with a calling that only you can fulfill. The strength you've built in your mind, body, and spirit was never meant to stay inside you. It was meant to overflow—into your family, your work, your community, and the Kingdom of God.

You now carry the tools. You've been given the framework. You've seen what's possible when belief meets discipline, when movement meets meaning, and when passion aligns with purpose.

The world doesn't need another passive observer. The world needs a warrior. A servant-leader.

A man or woman who walks boldly in faith, relentlessly pursues purpose, and lifts others along the way.

Let the excuses die here.

Let the old you be buried in the past.

Let today be the day you choose extraordinary strength.

Not just for your sake, but for everyone who's waiting on the other side of your obedience.

This is your time.

This is your calling.

This is your moment to live the life God created you for.

Step up. Stand tall.

And step fully into the extraordinary you.

Live Extraordinary.

Acknowledgments

First and foremost, I thank God—for His relentless grace, mercy, and guidance. Thank you Lord for the life you blessed me with and for guiding me to write this book. Without Him, none of this would be possible.

To my family—your love, patience, and encouragement through the highs and lows of this journey have been my foundation. You believed in me when I needed it most and reminded me daily why this mission matters.

To my wife Lori Beth, thank you for being my partner in life, love, and calling. Thank you for walking beside me in faith and purpose. Your strength, support, and partnership have carried me through every high and low. You are a living example of grace and grit.

To my daughter Kinley, you are one of the greatest blessings of my life and one of my greatest inspirations. I pray this book helps lay a path for the kind of world I hope you grow up in—one filled with strength, purpose, and grace. My prayer is that this book creates a legacy of strength and purpose that one day inspires you to pursue your own with courage and joy.

To DJ and Scott—thank you for believing in this mission and for walking beside me as co-owners, leaders, and brothers in the trenches. Your support, encouragement, and shared vision have been instrumental in building what we've created together—not only in business, but in impact.

To Martin Rooney—thank you your inspiration, coaching, and for building such an incredible program that changes and saves lives, including my own. Without you and TFW being placed in my life, this wouldn't be possible.

To Derek Sanford—thank you for your leadership, guidance, and the amazing church you have. Without you, your team, and all of Grace Church, I would not have had the actionable steps to grow closer to God and serve Him. Thank you for being an incredible conduit of the Holy Spirit and always overflowing to others.

To my incredible team—you are the heartbeat of health. Your dedication, your passion, and your commitment to making everyone you come in contact with healthy is nothing short of extraordinary. You inspire me every day, and I am beyond grateful to lead alongside you.

To my friends and mentors—you know who you are—thank you for sharpening me, challenging me, and walking alongside me through this vision. Your encouragement helped make this book possible.

To the entire Training for Warriors and Erie Fitness Academy famila—thank you for living this mission out loud. Your passion, discipline, and commitment to growth are proof that extraordinary strength is found in real people doing the work daily.

And to my mom—this book wouldn't exist without you. Thank you for making me the man that I am today. Your courage, your fight, and your unshakable love are embedded in every page. Watching you face cancer with resilience and faith showed me what true strength really looks like. Your life gave this message a heartbeat. You continue to inspire me, guide me, and remind me of the power of living with purpose, love, grace, and grit. I hope I've honored you with these words and the life that I live each day.

And finally, to you—the reader. Thank you for trusting me to walk this journey with you. You are why this book was written. My prayer is that it awakened something inside you. That it stirred your soul. That it called you higher. And that you now walk forward—not just stronger, but more aligned with the person God created you to be. This is not just a book. It's a mission. A calling. A movement. And I'm thankful you're part of it.

I'd Be Honored to Hear From You!

Thank you so much for taking this journey with me and for investing your time in Extraordinary Strength. Your thoughts and experiences mean the world to me—they help me grow as a writer and encourage others to step into their own extraordinary lives.

If this book inspired, challenged, or empowered you in any way, would you take just two minutes to leave a review on Amazon?

Your feedback not only shapes future editions and books but also helps more people discover this message of faith, strength, and purpose.

Thank you for being part of this mission—and for helping others find their extraordinary strength too.

With gratitude and strength,

Giordano Nunemaker

About the Author

Giordano "Gio" Nunemaker is on a mission to change and save lives—physically and spiritually. A passionate coach, speaker, and founder of The Extraordinary Strength Method™, Gio is dedicated to helping people build unbreakable strength—from the inside out. After battling depression, identity crises, and heartbreak, Gio discovered that true strength isn't built in the gym alone—it's forged in the trenches of life's struggles, grounded in faith, and fueled by purpose.

Born and raised in Cambridge Springs, Pennsylvania, Gio's journey wasn't always defined by faith. After first meeting Jesus at camp as a young man, he later walked away from his faith in college, reaching a rock bottom so dark he contemplated taking his own life. But through God's grace, the love of his wife, and rediscovering his spiritual foundation, Gio transformed his pain into purpose.

A lifelong athlete at heart, Gio played football in high school and volleyball in college, learning the power of teamwork and the necessity of individual accountability. Inspired early on by a gym teacher who taught him the power of belief and resilience, Gio's passion for sports led him to pursue a career in physical education. However, after experiencing the limitations of traditional systems and confronting deep personal setbacks, he realized his true calling: to empower others to become the extraordinary version of themselves God created them to be.

Competing in powerlifting and strongman taught him that true results come only through resilience and doing the work no one else can do for you—a lesson he now imparts to his community daily. His life and messages are dedicated to helping people reclaim joy, embrace discomfort, and live boldly on mission.

As Vice President and Head Coach of Erie Fitness Academy (EFA) & Training for Warriors South Erie, Gio oversees all programs and coaches, including the life-changing Training for Warriors group. Through EFA and his speaking engagements, Gio empowers people to transform their mind, body, spirit, and purpose—one choice and one action at a time. His guiding belief is to help every person he meets grow stronger in mind, body, spirit, and purpose—empowering them to own their story, awaken the extraordinary strength inside them, and become the extraordinary version of themselves.

Gio holds a degree in Human Performance from Edinboro University (2014) and is certified through TFW, USA Weightlifting, and as a CSCS. A champion of Extreme Ownership (his favorite EFA core value), he leads by example both in the gym and in life.

When he isn't coaching or writing, Gio loves spending time outdoors—shooting sporting clays, hunting, hiking with his wife Lori Beth, working on vehicles and toys, competing in strongman events, and playing sports. He lives in Union City, Pennsylvania, with his wife and daughter Kinley, joyfully awaiting their second daughter in September 2025.

His favorite book, Unbroken by Laura Hillenbrand, mirrors his own story: one of resilience, redemption, and unyielding faith.

Favorite scriptures that guide his journey include Romans 8:28, James 1:2–4, and Ephesians 2:10. As Martin Rooney says, "The greatest thing you can do with all your strength is to lift others up."

Connect with Gio and join the movement at ExtraordinaryStrengthMethod.com

Live Extraordinary.

www.ingramcontent.com/pod-product-compliance
Lightning Source LLC
Chambersburg PA
CBHW071136130626
46553CB00004B/1397